WISDOM IN THE OLD TESTAMENT TRADITIONS

DONN F. MORGAN

John Knox Press
ATLANTA

A portion of this manuscript appeared in a previously published essay, "Wisdom and the Prophets," *Studia Biblica 1978, JSOT* Supplement Series, 11, pp. 209-244, Sheffield, 1979. Used by permission.

Library of Congress Cataloging in Publication Data

Morgan, Donn F.
   Wisdom in the Old Testament traditions.

   Bibliography: p.
   Includes indexes.
   1. Wisdom literature. I. Title.
BS1455.M67   221'.06   80-84653
ISBN 0-8042-0188-9   AACR2
ISBN 0-8042-0189-7 (pbk.)

To Bruce

PREFACE

My interest in the interrelationship between the Old Testament wisdom literature and the rest of the Old Testament began many years ago while studying Psalm 111. That psalm, generally not considered a wisdom psalm, contains many elements usually associated with wisdom teaching. It appeared to me then that such a psalm reflected a closer and more complicated relationship between the sages and the cult than was usually assumed. Subsequent investigation led me to a vast scholarly literature and a debate over every aspect of the relationship between wisdom and the rest of the Old Testament. One disorienting factor was the absence of any study which attempted to examine this scholarship holistically, in an effort to determine the implications of this research for an overall view of wisdom and Israelite religion. It is part of my purpose to present such an overview, in the hopes that it may provide one starting point for continuing explorations. Although it would be virtually impossible to cite and discuss all the important works in this area, the notes and bibliography do provide an entry into the debate over wisdom and its place in the Old Testament.

It is with much fear and trepidation that I confess the primary purpose of this study is more than simply a history of research. The implications of finding wisdom in virtually all Old Testament literature suggest that a history of the wise men is possible, through an examination of their teachings in other major literary traditions. For a long time any focus on the wisdom tradition in Israel and its history has centered on wisdom literature itself. It is my belief that only by examining wisdom teachings and literary forms in other parts of the Old Testament will we be able to discover more fully the nature and scope of the wisdom tradition. This study, then, is a small step in that direction. I am aware that much more needs to be done, especially in the application of sociological and anthropological categories to this problem. Much remains unclear, but, I trust, the integral role of the wise in the message of the Old Testament will motivate further study in this important area. The problems raised (epistemological, historical, and theological) are of vital significance to all who are heirs of the biblical tradition and who are engaged in biblical theology.

I would not have been able to complete this study without the support and encouragement of many. I wish to thank Andrew W. Mellon and the Arthur Vining Davis Foundations for their support through a grant given by the Association of Theological Schools. It helped make possible a sabbatical year at Cambridge University where much of the research for this study was completed. I am grateful to the Church Divinity School of the Pacific and my colleagues there for their patience and encouragement in many different ways. I am much in debt to Walter Brueggemann, James Crenshaw, and R. N. Whybray for their careful reading of the manuscript and their helpful comments and suggestions. I wish also to thank Esther Davis for her editorial suggestions and her willingness to type a not always clear manuscript. Without the constant support and encouragement of my wife, Alda, in too many ways to mention, this study would never have been completed. Finally, because the ideas which motivated this project began and were developed in my teaching, I wish to thank all my students who questioned and encouraged me as I struggled with a difficult subject. It is to one of those, Bruce, who shared with me both enthusiasm and frustration, that I dedicate this book.

CONTENTS

Wisdom in the Old Testament Traditions

CHAPTER I
INTRODUCTION

The wisdom literature of the Old Testament and the traditions responsible for its creation and transmission have received much attention in biblical studies of the recent past.[1] There are many reasons for this, some to be related to ongoing tasks of biblical scholarship alone, others to changes occurring throughout theological study. Continuing forays into the study of literary forms, and the quest for ancient Near Eastern parallels to the wisdom literature are partially responsible. The difficulty of placing the message of wisdom literature into a synthetic schema which organizes Old Testament theology has also motivated proposals for more satisfactory arrangements. Coupled with these ongoing tasks in biblical studies, however, has been the breakdown of monolithic patterns used to describe not simply particular traditions but the nature and process of Israelite religion itself. As prophetic and priestly movements can no longer be separated easily from each other, so the conception of wisdom as a movement epistemologically and sociologically separable from other traditions in the New Testament is increasingly difficult to maintain. The growing tendency to explain the development of Israelite religion on the basis of a pluralistic matrix is not unique to Old Testament studies, but is reflected in the increasing use of Bauer's hypothesis in the New Testament as well, and may be found also in historical and theological studies.[2] Further manifestations of this turn away from orthodoxy to pluralism are the purported demise of neo-orthodoxy and one of its children, the biblical theology movement. This breakdown is often associated with an increased interest in the "secular." It is, therefore, not surprising that the theological characteristics of wisdom so often considered to be secular, especially when contrasted with other non-wisdom traditions, should receive more attention at this time.

Given these developments, this increased attention to wisdom literature and its relationship to other biblical traditions can therefore be viewed as the result of much larger shifts within the theological enterprise as a whole. The emphasis on the "secular" nature and concerns of wisdom is at least partially related to a movement away from a revelation-centered theology. Connected to the demise of neo-orthodoxy, it is often seen as an attempt to provide another biblical model for the doing of theology. What is important to stress at this point is that such an emphasis on "secular" is in fact simply a return to the natural versus revealed religion debates which were central to the birth of neo-orthodoxy itself. That is, the same dichotomies of reason versus revelation, nature versus history, et al., are operative. Only our evaluations of them have changed.

A focus on the interrelatedness of wisdom with other traditions, without necessarily attempting to find one or more traditions as theologically normative, is the other important direction in which wisdom studies are pointed. In this development the distinctive character of the biblical traditions is not to be found in the cult, the prophets, or any other particular movement, but rather in a total process witnessed to by their interrelationship. After the pluralistic model has been defined, the search for a historical, sociological, and especially theological matrix out of which it operates is extremely important. It is probably true that both of these developments are needed to explain the biblical traditions fully. While the normative focus on "revelation" or "reason" is not fair to all of the biblical witness, the differentiation of particular traditions represented by such dichotomies is necessary if a serious attempt is to be made to interrelate the traditions. On the other hand, it must be seriously questioned whether contemporary epistemological dichotomies, such as reason-revelation, are operative in the biblical texts themselves.

The focus on wisdom literature in the context of such developments is a natural one, for any effort to assess the Old Testament as a whole must surely take seriously this literature and attempt to relate it to the complex sociological, historical, and theological matrix which is Israelite religion and which produced the Old Testament. The emphasis in biblical studies on a pluralistic milieu for the growth of both individual traditions and Israelite religion as a whole has parallels not only in other academic disciplines, but also in contemporary society. Related to such scholarly trends are the collapse of melting pot ideologies and the emergence of movements stressing identity based on the particular rather than the common. To be sure, our view of minorities, women, and wisdom, for example, have been governed too much by orthodox ideologies which most often represent only one segment of the whole, usually the most powerful. Consequently, the individuality of the parts is obscured, depriving many of the power and recognition they deserve. Furthermore, the rich and multifaceted texture of the whole is also lost. On the other hand, exclusive or even primary stress on individuality, on personal or group identity, threatens losing sight of the pluralistic matrix which binds us together, culturally, historically, theologically. If the increased study of wisdom opens a new understanding of this tradition and its relationship to other Old Testament traditions, the implications of such understanding will hopefully aid us in other areas in which contemporary theology is concerned.

Having described an ultimately promising trend in biblical studies, it must be admitted that to date much of the research devoted to wisdom has failed to provide new paths toward the goal of understanding wisdom within the overall development of

Israelite religion, pluralistically conceived. Rather, at the present time there are several different notions about the historical and theological development of wisdom, no one definition of wisdom capable of winning consensus, much disagreement about the social setting and class of wisdom, and a lack of unanimity about the nature and development of some fundamental literary forms in wisdom literature.

The reasons for such confusion in wisdom studies stem at least partially from the nature of the wisdom literature itself. The absence of easily datable texts and explicit connections with other traditions makes it necessary for surmise. As has often been noted, our conception of the development of wisdom usually controls our analysis of the wisdom literature, rather than coming from it! Ancient Near Eastern parallels are often suspect, especially when clear references in or outside of the wisdom literature which would answer some of the questions above do not occur. As one recent commentator has stated, "caution is the watchword" when attempting to assess external influence upon wisdom literature.[3] It must be admitted, however, that much of the popularity of wisdom results not from a desire to integrate it into any pluralistic conception of Israelite religion, but rather because it provides an alternative to traditions usually considered revelational. It has thus been used to provide biblical warrant for emphases on the secular, rather than to witness to the inseparable combination of secular and religious perspectives in biblical theology.

In one area alone, a great many gains seem, at first glance, to have been made. Though we have been unable to define the nature, history, class, et al., of wisdom to everyone's satisfaction, there have been many recent studies which have claimed that the influence of wisdom can be found throughout the Old Testament.[4] This phenomenon in biblical studies is viewed with surprise and reservation by many who are aware of the uncertainties surrounding wisdom literature itself.[5] They find it difficult to understand how the "influence" of such a vaguely characterized entity can be so easily asserted. Puzzling and perhaps foolhardy as such attempts may be, it is this attempt to relate wisdom to other traditions through evidence partially provided by non-wisdom traditions themselves which is the starting point of this study. Such attempts to find and delineate wisdom throughout the Old Testament may be the most difficult to assess in terms of a positive contribution to wisdom studies and the history of Israelite religion, but they also offer the most promise.[6] To be sure, the nature of the interrelationship between traditions in ancient Israel cannot always be explained in terms of precise historical settings or theological motivations. Nevertheless, we may not only learn about the individual traditions themselves by studying this interrelationship, but we are also far less likely to isolate them from the rest of the biblical message—a danger which is surely inherent in the study of particular traditions alone. Thus the question of wisdom and its influence or presence in other areas of Israelite religion raises the issues of the common bond shared by all, sociologically and theologically, as well as the uncommon, that which distinguishes it from other traditions and provides a special value and identity for it. Surely this is important not only for wisdom but for all of contemporary society as it struggles to find its component and corporate identities.

According to some scholars, wisdom influence is to be found in almost every non-wisdom literary tradition in the Old Testament. The criteria for determining this influence are varied. Examples cited to demonstrate "influence" have included the use of vocabulary and theological concerns peculiar to the wise men, references to experiential knowledge, allusions to the "wise," the presence of literary forms commonly associated with wisdom, geographical references, and many others. While there has been no unanimity about a basic working definition of wisdom influence, there has been a consensus among many scholars that such influence does exist and is widespread. Not surprisingly, such assertions have been subject to severe and penetrating criticism, primarily methodological in nature. Crenshaw, Murphy, and Whybray, for example, have been more concerned with the logic of conclusions reached on the basis of the evidence cited. Crenshaw has maintained that much of so-called wisdom influence can be explained by assuming a common lexical stock for the literary traditions of the Old Testament. For example, theological conceptions and vocabulary seen as peculiar to Proverbs but also found in Genesis 3 are not necessarily peculiar to one tradition but rather common to many. More importantly, many studies maintaining wisdom influence are guilty of circular reasoning, by assuming what is to be proved. For example, to find wisdom in Genesis one first posits its potential existence there, searches for biblical texts to demonstrate it, and, naturally, defines what is found as "wisdom."

Both of the above criticisms and others must be taken seriously when attempting to evaluate the extent and implications of wisdom influence in the Old Testament. It must be admitted that sometimes the influence of the wisdom tradition has been maintained without carefully examining other possibilities. The attempt to relate the implications of wisdom influence to a sociological, historical reality compatible with wisdom literature itself is one example. Nevertheless, the lack of consensus about many major issues involved in the wisdom literature, as noted above, is surely one reason why a clear relationship between wisdom influence and wisdom is difficult. Moreover, the insistence upon wisdom literature as the starting point for any discussion of the tradition and a continuing belief that much of it must be dated in the post-exilic period make it difficult to place the wisdom tradition within a pluralistic matrix for all of Israelite religion. On the one hand, we don't know enough about the roots of the tradition responsible for the literature and much of the literature appears late in the history of Israelite religion. On the other hand, because of this we are unable to find influence of this tradition elsewhere in the Old Testament and questions of interrelationship and reciprocal growth are difficult to answer. We are, therefore, at a stalemate, with impatience on both sides of the question.

One purpose of this study is to suggest a possible way out of this stalemate, in the hopes that the history and development of the wisdom tradition may ultimately be seen more clearly. We agree that the wisdom tradition and its "influence" in other non-wisdom literature must be related to the wisdom literature itself, especially when questions of definition and theological conceptions peculiar to the tradition are discussed. The methodological difficulties involved whenever wisdom influence is discerned must also be recognized and their implications for its validity must be evaluated. Nevertheless, despite some recent significant studies of the social setting and development of the wisdom tradition, it appears that the wisdom literature by itself will not be able to provide a picture of this tradition which will disclose its relationship with regard to other major traditions in the Old Testament.

The suggestion and working hypothesis of this study is a simple one. In order to break out of the present stalemate, we must assess holistically the implications of recent scholarship maintaining the influence of wisdom. The possibility that this influence is indicative of several important sociological, historical, and theological interfaces between wisdom and other traditions in Israelite religion must be considered. These interfaces or points of contact, *when viewed as a whole,* may provide us with important insights into the nature and development of the wisdom tradition which a focus on wisdom literature alone cannot. The goal of this study then is to trace the development of the wisdom tradition in ancient Israel, utilizing wisdom influence in evinced and studied non-wisdom texts as a major source and indication of this development. Though further study of both wisdom influence and the wisdom literature itself is called for, perhaps some of the implications found in the holistic overview presented here may stimulate new questions and answers.

It is not the purpose of this study to evaluate each study of wisdom influence from a critical methodological perspective and then to determine whether or not it can be used to support the picture of the wisdom tradition being proposed. Rather, significant proposals and biblical texts will all be presented, though surely some are more convincing than others. It is, however, possible that when all the wisdom influence is examined the methodological questions will be placed in perspective, allowing them to have more validity in some instances, less in others. Otherwise, if methodology becomes the only criterion for assessing the relationship of wisdom to other traditions in the Old Testament, then we are paralyzed, unable to make any assertions or to move beyond these issues to larger, potentially more important ones. Despite the risks involved, the goal of learning more about wisdom and the nature of ancient Israelite society seems to make them worth taking.

The Wisdom Tradition

All discussions of wisdom must at some point reach a moment of truth, a time when whatever is meant by this designation must be defined. This is hazardous, for the definition and description may be so amorphous as to be meaningless, or so specific as not to be helpful in discussing much of the biblical material associated with it. Most are agreed that wisdom is a process, a living tradition, and *any* definition to a certain extent reifies this phenomenon and therefore makes assumptions of continued growth and interrelationship with other traditions difficult to explain. Nevertheless, it is necessary to examine briefly some of the current definitions of wisdom, interrelating whatever insights may be had from non-wisdom literature, in order to ascertain exactly what wisdom in non-wisdom literature might reflect and how it is to be related to wisdom literature itself.

There are two issues involved in defining the nature and scope of the wisdom tradition, or any other tradition for that matter. On the one hand, a tradition must have certain characteristics which *distinguish* it from others, which give it an identity and integrity of its own. Although scholars continue to debate at what point the wisdom tradition becomes "religious" and "theological," or the origin of the proverbial admonition or sentence, nevertheless particular teachings and literary forms found in the wisdom literature itself usually form the basis of this tradition's distinctiveness. On the other hand, it is usually the case that major traditions in any culture are *interrelated,* and this phenomenon has become important in defining the nature of the society. The presence of wisdom in the non-wisdom literature witnesses primarily to the interrelatedness of the wisdom tradition rather than to its distinctiveness. Because of this, many have chosen to speak of a "common cultural stock" which is no longer useful in defining the nature or direct influence of wisdom but rather witnesses to a secondary development after the particular and distinctive teachings of the tradition have become public property. Others go further and state such a tradition was *always* public property, never belonging to a sociologically definable and distinct group.

But another possibility exists. At times vocabulary, theological concepts, and especially direct references to particular groups (e.g., the *ḥakamim,* "the wise") make clear that a very specific entity which might be called the "wisdom tradition" is being referred to. If only these texts are examined, reconstructions like that of McKane, focusing on the rationalistic, empirical nature of the tradition, are possible and related to the always amenable wisdom literature for its justification.[7] At this point we would suggest a compromise, one which takes seriously both the distinctive nature of the tradition as well as its interrelatedness to other traditions. By focusing upon the non-wisdom literature, we may begin with those passages which reflect definite knowledge of and (usually) conflict with advocates of wisdom perspectives.

Once this evidence has been recognized, the possibility, even the probability (unless we choose on the basis of contemporary epistemological, theological dichotomies to exclude it) that the wisdom tradition has been a contributing factor in other parts of biblical traditions becomes a serious consideration. Other areas of non-wisdom literature which appear to reflect concerns in common with wisdom are then capable of aiding us in our definition of wisdom. We may eventually need to view passages associated with wisdom perspectives in non-wisdom texts as part of a cultural stock, but nevertheless two important observations can be made. First, a particular and distinctive wisdom tradition existed in Israel. Second, its interrelationship with other traditions makes it dangerous to assume its character can or should be defined only or even primarily on the basis of direct references to the wise or wisdom. Thus, while wisdom literature remains the basis for our evaluation of and comparison with non-wisdom literature, a complete picture of the tradition must take seriously the observations made about its presence in this non-wisdom literature.[8]

Wisdom has been defined in many ways. Until recently it was usually identified with monarchical officials, "schools," and even a particular educated class. Most often it was seen as empirical and rational, relying on experiential authority, separated from other traditions focused on revelational history, cultic practices and concerns, etc. Some of these definitions continue to be espoused, and indeed must be if the distinctiveness of wisdom is to be maintained. Recent studies of wisdom in non-wisdom literature have broadened our conception of the tradition, however. It is now sometimes spoken of as a movement, a way of life, a way of thought and speech, to be found in the clan or family as well as in the institutions of the monarchy. Through his rigorous methodological critiques of such studies, Crenshaw especially has raised this possibility to the fore. Asserting a fairly rigid definition of wisdom stemming from the wisdom literature alone, Crenshaw suggests much so-called wisdom influence is simply reflective of common concerns shared by prophet, priest, and sage in Israel. While not necessarily dependent upon Crenshaw, the following statements are reflective of a change in mood, which still wishes to compare and study constructively "wisdom and" and "in" non-wisdom literature while avoiding the difficult problems of provenance, intention, and dependence, rightly questioned by Crenshaw.

It is not a question of the direct influence of the sages or of the wisdom literature, but rather of an approach to reality which was shared by all Israelites in varying degrees. The teachers were of course the experts, particularly sensitive to the insights that experience offered, and upon which conduct was to be based. But the existence of experts even presupposes that the average Israelite shared to some extent in the sapiential understanding of reality (which was, without doubt, not alien to Yahwism to them).[9]

I am concerned more broadly with the whole way in which an established community of opinion preserves, discerns, knows and decides. Wisdom both affirms and presents a critique of this unexamined intellectual climate. It is my impression that scholarship may miss these urgent issues if it focuses on narrow and precise definitions and misses the epistemological crisis. My approach here addresses what Crenshaw calls "wisdom thinking."[10]

Our concern is not to trace in Isa. 40-55 specific terms, propositions, or literary forms that are deemed characteristic of the wisdom literature itself, much less to search for traces of the influence of an alleged "wisdom school." We are concerned here only with the general intellectual situation which is mirrored in the canonical wisdom books.[11]

It is, of course, true that wisdom perceptions have been widely disseminated and have, occasionally, found expression in the presentation of history. But that is not at all surprising, for these teachings did not arise from any secret doctrine but became part of the common cultural stock. More than elsewhere, this way of thinking seems to have permeated the presentation of the Succession Narrative, which was certainly written by someone at Solomon's court. In spite of this, the religious problem and the objective of these works was different.[12]

In all of the above positions, there is still a serious attempt to define the wisdom tradition in a very specific, distinctive manner, even if attempts to find this wisdom in non-wisdom literature occur less frequently. There is, however, a position more radical than this, which examines the wisdom literature itself and all wisdom influenced texts, and which does not find enough sociological and theological distinctiveness to warrant significant separation from other traditions.

> . . . There existed an educated class, albeit a small one, of well-to-do citizens who were accustomed to read for edification and for pleasure, and from among them there arose from time to time men of literary ability and occasionally of genius who provided the literature which sastified their demand. . . . They constituted a tradition only in the sense that they concerned themselves more than the majority of their contemporaries in an intellectual way with the problems of human life.[13]

> What justifies associating this ever-growing range of Old Testament material in a common tradition is neither a similar theological purpose nor a fixed literary genre, but rather, an identifiable intellectual stance and literary idiom, which stem from a common educational background. The "Wisdom" tradition of the Old Testament is no more or no less than the "classical" tradition of its educated men.[14]

> . . . One needs rather to look for a common religious tradition in early Israel from which prophets, priests and wise men selected specific emphases without necessarily rejecting those emphases chosen by the other groups.[15]

We will not apply and discuss the methodological critiques of Crenshaw, Whybray, and others to all of the texts examined. Serious consideration of them, however, often makes it difficult to utilize wisdom influence in order to assert authorship or influence of the wise in non-wisdom literature. In fact, as we shall see, "influence" appears often the wrong term, the wrong explanation. Our starting point in attempting to discuss the presence of the wisdom tradition will be wisdom literature. Often, to be sure, no explicit parallels can be made. Nevertheless, beginning with those texts which contain certain forms or teachings primarily associated with the wisdom literature, the non-wisdom literature points to a use of wisdom which seems to indicate more than simply a "common cultural stock," although it is surely that as well. In a variety of social settings, the non-wisdom traditions (prophetic, priestly, et al.)

borrow and utilize wisdom perspectives and are ultimately partially responsible for the growth and development of the tradition itself! Such an observation makes two conclusions possible. Either the common cultural stock was itself the "tradition" whereupon the primary carriers of the tradition are prophets, priests, etc.; or there existed a group, yet to be defined fully, whose teachings and forms were indeed dispersed throughout Israelite society and utilized by all. In the latter instance it would be difficult to maintain influence, perhaps, but the distinctiveness of origin (literary and theological) often remains. Furthermore, the dialogue which occurs at this popular level is one important factor in the future thought of the sages. It is this latter view we endorse here, primarily on the basis of the wisdom literature itself and the relationship of non-wisdom traditions to it.

The following working hypotheses assume the existence of a wisdom tradition in Israel and provide guidelines for our study. First, the wisdom tradition is responsible for the wisdom literature found in the Old Testament (Proverbs, Job, Ecclesiastes, a few psalms). Therefore literary forms and the social and theological perspectives which have their provenance and occur primarily in this literature should form the foundation for any discussion of the nature, scope, and particular perspectives of the wisdom tradition. Second, the wisdom tradition is responsible, directly or indirectly, for the wisdom influence found in non-wisdom literature of the Old Testament. Since the means of transmission is not always or easily determined, the possibility of indirect or secondary influence may be assumed. Third, the wisdom tradition has at least one sociological base, that is, a means by which its literature and world-view is communicated. The sociological base is in all probability to be found in close proximity to the bases for other traditions, even interrelated with them (the monarchy, cult, etc.). Fourth, the theological perspectives of the wisdom tradition are different from, but not necessarily incompatible with, those of other non-wisdom traditions, even when wisdom and other traditions appear to be in conflict. Fifth, the wisdom tradition is assumed to be present in Israel from at least the early monarchical period. Sixth, the wisdom tradition is present in a "popular" form, perhaps to be associated with the family/clan structure. Literary remnants of this form of the wisdom tradition may or may not be discerned in Old Testament wisdom literature itself.

Wisdom Influence

As noted above, the use of the word "influence" to describe certain literary and theological characteristics of wisdom within non-wisdom texts is problematic. On the one hand, influence does at least point to a distinct phenomenon, having its origin outside the provenance of the particular literature being examined. On the other hand, "influence" seems to indicate that in some way this tradition is intruding, finding a place for its perspective regardless of a basically different stance. We would maintain that this latter picture of the wisdom tradition is incompatible with the evidence. It is better to suggest that the wisdom tradition, though perhaps different in origin from other traditions, reflects one of many ways used to perceive the actions of Yahweh by ancient Israel and their implications for individual and community. The presence of wisdom in non-wisdom texts does not therefore witness to a combination of two or more epistemologically and theologically separable traditions. On the contrary, it points to a way of theologizing which utilized many different perspectives in an effort to find the common, Yahwistic matrix or thread behind all experience. While we will, primarily for the sake of continuity with previous scholarship being presented below, continue to use the word "influence" to describe those places where evidence of the wisdom tradition has been found, it is important to recognize its limitations.

Any definition of wisdom influence must be compatible with the broad conception of the wisdom tradition stated above. Therefore, whenever possible, the provenance of wisdom influence is to be sought in wisdom literature. Wisdom influence cannot be generically incompatible with the wisdom tradition's major characteristics as found in wisdom literature. Nevertheless, we may expect wisdom influence to be reflected in literary forms, theology, etc., which have been modified by their contact with other traditions. However, the function and the historical, sociological bases presupposed must retain some definite relationship to the fundamental characteristics of the wisdom tradition. General appeals to experiential learning are not sufficient evidence for wisdom in a particular passage. The theological perspectives and literary forms associated with wisdom should betray their origin but at the same time not be bound by a definition which does not allow for change and adaptation. A distinction between wisdom "influence" and "wisdom "contact" may at times be helpful in evaluating the implications of scholarly research. Wisdom contact may be found in texts which manifest similarities to or direct knowledge of the wisdom tradition but which are far removed from that tradition in the light of particular adaptation. Examples of such contact might be stylistic phenomena or direct reference to the wise. While both influence and contact can be helpful in tracing the development of the wisdom tradition, the former is most significant in attempting to determine the characteristics of the tradition inside and outside the wisdom literature itself.

Finally, the historical, sociological, and theological development of the wisdom tradition pointed to and implied by wisdom influence in non-wisdom literature must be compared and hopefully integrated into current theories of development stemming from wisdom literature itself. It must be recognized, however, that wisdom influence may itself contain the clues to developments seen but not verifiable in wisdom literature. That is, the use of the wisdom tradition in other traditions and the subsequent changes in theological perspectives brought about by such use may itself be partially responsible for further developments and changes within wisdom itself. Failure to recognize or accept this possibility has led to the stalemate concerning wisdom influence noted above. It has also presupposed a monolithic, static wisdom tradition which is *sui generis* and unable to be related significantly to other major voices in the Old Testament.

The history of the wisdom tradition which follows is based primarily on the evidence provided by the interrelationship with other major traditions; such a history is already implied by the vast amount of wisdom influence posited by recent bibilical research. The development will be traced chronologically. No doubt lacunae in our knowledge of the wisdom tradition will continue to exist, even if all the implications of wisdom influence were synthesized. Nevertheless, there are many important reasons why the present study is necessary. First, such an approach to the wisdom literature may indeed be a way out of the methodological quagmire in which we find ourselves. Secondly, before future comprehensive and ground-breaking Old Testament theologies and histories of Israelite religion are to be formulated, a better picture of the individual traditions and their functions in a pluralistic-heterodox matrix (versus monolithic-orthodox) is necessary. Thirdly, if indeed our knowledge of the development of the wisdom tradition can be illuminated through a study of the interaction with other traditions usually considered to be not merely distinct but sometimes antithetical, our use (and abuse?) of several dichotomies to explain and categorize the perspectives of Old Testament traditions must be seriously questioned (including nature-grace, reason-revelation, nature-history, etc.). This might lead to Old Testament theologies which focus more on the integration of different but not incompatible traditions than on the use of biblical or extra-biblical categories which elevate certain perspectives and consign others to relative unimportance.

As noted above, the movement away from a neo-orthodoxy which stressed revelational concepts and categories may be related to two different developments within the study of wisdom literature itself. On the one hand, the theological perspectives of wisdom, understandably played down by theologians concerned with revelation, have provided an alternative way of doing theology, much at home in our "secular" world. On the other hand, the interrelationship between wisdom and revelation witnessed to by studies of wisdom influence points toward another, pluralistic, conception of biblical and contemporary theology. This latter model strongly questions the isolation of any tradition, revelational or not, maintaining that all theology needs to take seriously the different ways of perceiving God, man, and the world. The polarizing of reason and revelation is, according to the implications of these studies, not a step forward from archaic biblical world-views, but rather an impediment to the doing of theology which takes seriously all the dimensions of our experience. Perhaps we can learn from the wise and from the model of interaction and growth presupposed in this study by the history of their tradition. This may open the wisdom literature itself to more serious study and use in the church, not only in addition to but in relation to other literature of the Bible—in the theology, worship, and other areas of our common life.

CHAPTER II
WISDOM IN THE PRE-MONARCHICAL PERIOD

An examination of previous wisdom studies reveals little discussion pertaining to wisdom for the period before the monarchy. This is not surprising, indeed it is at least partially warranted by the quantity and nature of the textual evidence available. Virtually all of the texts which may contain wisdom forms, themes, and concerns are to be dated, in their present literary context at least, in the monarchical period or later. Moreover, proverbial forms, even when recognizable, are very difficult to date. The possibility of finding a setting capable of adequate temporal and sociological definition behind the present literary context is open to scepticism. Nevertheless, we have the presence of a number of simple proverbs and other wisdom forms, the existence of popular wisdom in both the ancient Near East and in all cultures, the assumption that an oral tradition precedes the literary form of many proverbs, and a conviction that the roots of wisdom instruction and its interrelationship with other societal institutions and concerns (especially law) are not to be found only in the institution of the monarchy. These have created a consensus among scholars that the origin of at least one strand of the wisdom tradition is to be found in the pre-monarchical period.[1]

There have been two primary focal points for the discussion of pre-monarchical wisdom. The first has been a development of the notion of popular wisdom, expressed in a number of wisdom forms, found throughout the Old Testament, which reflects a popular ethos in some way detached from (or unaffected by) the monarchy and the more complex forms and more theological (religious?) concerns which developed there. Here it is important to note that advocates of a popular pre-monarchical wisdom are rarely concerned with the setting for such wisdom. Rather, they confine their attention to the form and content of the sayings themselves.[2] The second focal point has been that of clan/family wisdom. The studies which discuss this phenomena have surely been concerned to discuss various formal aspects of this wisdom, but primary attention has been given to the ethos of the family/tribe which makes this particular setting compatible with the beginnings and development of one part of the wisdom tradition.[3] Other studies dependent upon the notion of a clan wisdom (for example, those of H. W. Wolff) have maintained that this setting and the teachings associated with it never became totally assimilated into the wisdom traditions associated with the monarchy. This, as we shall see, is perhaps the most dramatic difference between those who speak of popular wisdom and clan/family wisdom. In any case, despite these scholarly differences, the phenomena of popular and clan wisdom to a great extent are not only compatible with each other but point essentially to the same reality.

Before discussing popular and clan wisdom separately, it is important to clarify the presuppositions which are basic to any discussion of wisdom in this period. The lack of a concrete setting, regardless of the concern with family or clan, and the primary emphasis upon formal and thematic characteristics are revealing. They disclose an important aspect of our evaluation of wisdom, namely, that our notion of wisdom's development will determine our evaluation of the evidence we find. Thus we sometimes *assume,* for example, that popular wisdom must have less complex literary forms and be characterized by non-theological/"secular" concerns, while later wisdom will have more sophisticated literary conventions and will be more directly under the influence of a Yahwistic culture and world view. The examples of popular wisdom we find, therefore, will be those passages which, though incapable of precise dating or setting, manifest these characteristics. It is not our purpose to critique this type of procedure, for in view of the evidence itself it appears impossible to proceed in any other manner. Regardless of the fact that a notion of the development of wisdom is a presupposition for our categorization of pre-monarchical wisdom, the evidence cited below seems to justify such a presupposition. The peculiar interaction of wisdom and other traditions in Israelite society at this and later periods is ultimately better explained if some attention is paid to its pre-monarchical roots.

Popular Wisdom

Until recently the view put forth by Eissfeldt and others asserting the existence of a popular proverb sentence form, and, with it, the assumption of an ethos which produced a general, less sophisticated form of wisdom was taken for granted.[4] Lately, however, Hermisson, Murphy, and others have challenged this view, maintaining that there is no reason why the preoccupation with particular subjects should be considered "popular."[5] There is also considerable debate regarding the form of the popular proverb, whether it ever really had a prose form, whether a poetic form could exist outside a highly specialized context, etc. Scott and Crenshaw have reasserted their belief that a popular wisdom did indeed exist in pre-monarchical Israel, though the development of this type of wisdom in the later monarchical period is difficult to trace.[6] It would appear that the existence of popular sayings in non-wisdom traditions, many of which can be associated with similar sayings in the wisdom literature itself, is strong enough to justify the use of the term popular wisdom. The connotations of such a designation, however, should be directed toward the ethos which produced the literature so designated. It should not be assumed to indicate archaic forms or particular thematic concerns which have rightly been shown to be present in other settings as well.

Although much of the past discussion of popular wisdom has dealt with forms and concerns present in the Book of Proverbs, the present study will only allude to such texts, and center instead upon popular wisdom as manifested in non-wisdom literature which might be utilizing pre-monarchical traditions. The reason for this is twofold. First, there is little or no agreement concerning which texts in Proverbs might be popular and/or pre-monarchical. Second, the material in non-wisdom literature often has more significant indicators of its potential date. Moreover, it represents the type of literature with which this study has its primary concern, namely wisdom forms and concerns within literature governed by a theological perspective and tradition different from that usually associated with wisdom literature.

After assuming that popular sayings best categorized as wisdom exist in most societies, the discussion of popular wisdom invariably begins with an investigation of the meaning of the Hebrew word most often used to designate such sayings, *mašal*. As Eissfeldt and others after him have noted, regardless of the etymology and precise original meaning of the term, it is now applied to a number of different forms in the Old Testament, not all of which can be associated with a wisdom provenance. Eissfeldt believed that the various forms which *mašal* may refer to (instruction, discourse, literary wisdom saying, parable, oracle) are developments from the popular proverbial saying, *mašal* in its earliest, purest form. Surely Hermisson is correct when he asserts that didactic wisdom cannot be seen only in terms of a development from popular wisdom, though to deny the existence of such a development seems to go too far in the other direction. It is important to note that the designation "popular" and with it a potential pre-monarchical setting is often dependent upon the degree to which Eissfeldt's thesis or corollaries developed from it are accepted. Thus, for example, is the riddle to be considered a development from the *mašal* before or after the wisdom of the Old Testament was governed by the schools of the monarchy? If before, then it is popular wisdom; if after, then it must be considered the product of a tradition more closely associated with institutions of the state and not properly designated as "popular."

The following presentation of some examples of popular wisdom is not all-inclusive, nor does it prejudge the decisions made about the history of wisdom forms by experts in the field. It is simply a list of sayings for which there is some evidence of a popular origin and ethos in the pre-monarchical period. A developmental theory of forms should be contingent upon such a study rather than the basis for it.

Proverbs. The basic form of the popular proverb is much debated, but the following are examples of this genre cited by many different scholars.

> He was a mighty hunter before the Lord; therefore it is said, *"Like Nimrod, a mighty hunter before the Lord."* (Gen. 10:9)

> You shall take no bribe, *for a bribe blinds the officials and subverts the cause of those who are in the right.* (Exod. 23:8)

> Therefore it became a proverb, *"Is Saul also among the prophets?"* (1 Sam. 10:12, cf. 1 Sam. 19:24)

> *"The Lord sees not as man sees; man looks on the outward appearance, but the Lord looks on the heart."* (1 Sam. 16:7)

> Therefore it is said, *"The blind and the lame shall not come into the house."* (2 Sam. 5:8)

> As the proverb of the ancients says, *"Out of the wicked comes forth wickedness."* (1 Sam. 24:13)

> *"Let not him that girds on his armor boast himself as he that puts it off."* (1 Kings 20:11)

> *"As the man is, so is his strength."* (Judg. 8:21)

> *"With the jawbone of an ass*
> *   heaps upon heaps;*
> *with the jawbone of an ass*
> *   have I slain a thousand men."* (Judg. 15:16)

Besides these passages the following texts have also been seen as examples of popular proverbs: Ezek. 16:44; Isa. 5:19; Zeph. 1:12; Jer. 23:28, 31:29; Ezek. 18:2, 12:22; Hos. 8:7; Amos 6:12; Ezek. 28:2. From the Book of Proverbs the following have been cited: Prov. 10:6, 11, 15; 18:11, 14; 20:19; 10:22; 11:2, 22, 27; 13:3; 14:23; 19:16; 14:4, 28; 17:16; 25:13, 19, 20, 25; 26:27; 27:3; as well as Job 2:4.

Very few generalizations can be made about popular proverbs on the basis of these texts alone. Some of them (e.g., 2 Sam. 20:18 and perhaps also 2 Sam. 5:8) appear to be popular in origin but fulfill no proverbial function, however, that might be defined.[7] Many of them are introduced with an almost etiological formula, "therefore, it is said," or its equivalent. In certain cases (e.g., 1 Sam. 10:12 and 19:24), it is quite clear the proverbial saying itself existed independently of literary context, being placed in its present position only secondarily. These passages and others would seem to confirm the existence of popular aphorisms which circulated throughout the populace, being used, as is the custom today, in a variety of contexts and for a number of purposes.

Parables. Nathan's parable to David has been cited as an example of wisdom and its presence in the Succession Narrative surely creates the possibility of a pre-monarchical origin.

> There were two men in a certain city, the one rich and the other poor. The rich man had very many flocks and herds; but the poor man had nothing but one little ewe lamb which he had bought. And he brought it up, and it grew up with him and his children; it used to eat of his morsel, and drink from his cup, and lie in his bosom, and it was like a daughter to him. Now there came a traveler to the rich man, and he was unwilling to take one of his own flock or herd to prepare for the wayfarer who had come to him, but he took the poor man's lamb, and prepared it for the man who had come to him.

The possibility that some form of 2 Sam. 12:1-4 circulated before the monarchy cannot be discounted, but the peculiarities of this text which might tell us more of the nature and concerns of the wisdom tradition at this time are far from clear. Nevertheless, the way of life referred to and the potential legal uses of this form (cf. Exod. 23:8) should be noted. The Song of the Vineyard in Isa. 5:1-7 has also been claimed as a parable and example of wisdom, though clearly in a period to be dealt with later.

Riddles. There is only one riddle in the Old Testament, Judges 14:14-18, though many have suggested that other passages, such as the numerical sayings in Prov. 30:21-31, are in fact answers to riddles.[8] In addition there is, of course, the reference to riddles posed by the Queen of Sheba to Solomon in 1 Kings 10:1. There are also a number of passing references to riddles which indicate the form was in common use in Israel (Ezek. 17:3ff., etc.).

> And he said to them,
> "Food came from the eater;
> Sweetness came from strength." (Judg. 14:14)[9]

Although the Book of Judges has been edited by the Deuteronomist, most commentaries have not automatically assigned the riddle to a later period than that of Samson, but have tried rather to puzzle out the meaning of the riddle itself. It has clearly been adapted to its present position, but in spite of that and in light of other forms of wisdom present in the pre-monarchical period, there seems to be no reason to believe this riddle or ones like it was not common in the earlier time.

Fables. Two important fables in the Old Testament both occur in non-wisdom literature (cf. also Isa. 10:15, 29:16). In 2 Kings 14:9 the fable appears to be out of context, for it does not seem an appropriate reply of Jehoash to Amaziah.[10] The second and more well-known fable is that of Jotham.

> The trees once went forth to anoint a king over them; and they said to the olive tree, "Reign over us." But the olive tree said to them, "Shall I leave my fatness, by which gods and men are honored, and go to sway over the trees?" And the trees said to the fig tree, "Come you, and reign over us." But the fig tree said to them, "Shall I leave

my sweetness and my good fruit, and go to sway over the trees?"
And the trees said to the vine, "Come you and reign over us." But
the vine said to them, "Shall I leave my wine which cheers gods and
men, and go to sway over the trees?" Then all the trees said to the
bramble, "Come you and reign over us." And the bramble said to
the trees, "If in good faith you are anointing me king over you, then
come and take refuge in my shade; but if not, let fire come out of the
bramble and devour the cedars of Lebanon." (Judg. 9:8-15)

One of the key issues regarding this passage is whether or not the
monarchy of Judah or Israel is presupposed. Many commentators
have asserted that the fable, at least until the introduction of the
bramble, is ancient, belonging to pre-monarchical times. Boling
believes that the bramble section is a later Yahwistic addition, but
not concerned with the monarchy as much as with the covenant.[11]
Lindars, in a creative and stimulating article, has suggested that v.
15 is an independent proverb attached to the original fable. More
important for our purposes, Lindars goes on to suggest that the
fable may have originated in the settlement period in a Canaanite
milieu as a social commentary of the people against an upstart
king.[12] The fable would then be addressed to those who had refused
kingship, thus bringing about the present situation. There seem to
be enough possibilities in the pre-monarchical period of Israel to
accept this period as the origin for the present text. Moreover, the
text witnesses to a veiled manner of speaking which can be
categorized as popular wisdom.

In addition to these major genres most often classified as
belonging to the wisdom tradition, a number of other *possible*
instances of pre-monarchical wisdom may be briefly mentioned.
Allegories (cf. e.g., Ezek. 17:3-8, 19:2-9, 10-14), though not found
in pre-monarchical texts, may indeed have been a part of popular
wisdom. Von Rad and others have also noted parallel thematic
concerns in Exod. 20:20 (fear of the LORD), Judg. 2:6–3:6
(retribution), and later texts (Hos. 4:9, etc.) which may indicate
early connections between wisdom and other traditions. Finally, B.

Childs has suggested that Exod. 1:8–2:10, the narrative of the birth of Moses, may be a historicized wisdom tale. He has compared it to the Joseph Story. Although the traditions behind this story are at least in part pre-monarchical, the story will be examined in the next chapter, since monarchical institutions are in some way responsible for its present form and context.

When all of the evidence for "popular wisdom" is assessed, what general characteristics can be assigned to this phenomenon? It seems unwarranted and unwise to deny the existence of such a phenomenon in view of the multiplicity of examples of the forms and concerns commonly associated with wisdom. But it also appears difficult to characterize the nature of this wisdom in broad developmental ways. While, for example, Scott is surely correct to maintain the existence of such a popular or folk wisdom, the patterns he describes as characteristic of such proverbs are not easily located in non-wisdom literature. Since a plausible case can be made for the existence of "popular" proverbs composed by the same circles responsible for more complex forms (fable, riddle, etc.), it seems best to affirm the presence of popular wisdom without assuming the simpler one-line form as necessary for this classification. In light of Judg. 9:8–15, 1 Sam. 16:7, and other sayings, it is also difficult to claim that earlier popular wisdom was individualistic while later wisdom focuses on the community and religious concerns. Perhaps the most that can be said, at this point, is that popular wisdom utilized a variety of forms, was invariably transmitted orally, and was retained and utilized in a number of settings which perceived its particular means of expression (and theology?) to be appropriate to its own purposes and worldview.

Although Lindars and others have suggested definite settings for some of the passages containing popular wisdom, by and large this is not the case. In view of the diversity of settings in which they are now found, we can only infer that these expressions were common to much of society. The precise means of transmission for this wisdom in the pre-monarchical period is not clearly identified. This is itself a clue to the nature of wisdom at this time, something "popular" and transmitted in particular forms, but which was not to be attributed to a formal institution in any official way. The one exception to this conclusion is the family/tribe/clan, and it is to this we must now turn.

Clan Wisdom

In many ways, the focus upon the family, tribe, or clan as the origin for wisdom is not new.[13] Surely those who have found popular wisdom in the pre-monarchical period have made reference to the family as a possible locus for such wisdom. But the new emphasis upon the family or clan by Audet, Gerstenberger, and others is filled with far more implications for the development of wisdom and the history of Israelite religion than is the notion of a general, popular wisdom. First of all, those who have discussed clan wisdom recently begin with form-critical observations which do not focus on the disparate wisdom forms with possible pre-monarchical origins discussed above as popular wisdom. Rather, the studies examine and compare admonitions (Mahnwörter) and thematic concerns of wisdom literature with the forms and concerns of Israelite law. The similarities found in form and content are subsequently discussed in terms of how law functions in clan societies and the type of society needing laws such as found in the Pentateuch. Ultimately this new emphasis upon clan wisdom is important and needs to be differentiated from theories concerning popular wisdom for two reasons. First, the texts studied and compared with wisdom literature are significantly different, not to be associated with the genres of wisdom literature in their present form, but rather considered in terms of the ethos from which they may have come. Second, the societal matrix which is utilized to explain the formal similarities between wisdom and law is different from that of popular wisdom (which for the most part needs no particular societal presuppositions at all). This second reason may be extremely important in understanding the nature and growth of one part of the wisdom tradition throughout the history of Israelite religion.[14]

Although Gerstenberger and Richter were the first to study and compare the formal elements of prohibitions in the law and in the wisdom literature, two important studies by Gemser and Audet provide an earlier introduction to this area. Gemser, in studying the form and content of the motive clauses attached to the laws in the Pentateuch, concluded that an archaic element lay behind the present form of these clauses. Noting, for example, the proverbial nature of Exod. 23:8 (cf. Deut. 16:19), "a bribe blinds the officials, and subverts the cause of those who are in the right," he saw "a striking example of the intrinsic coherence of legal practice and wisdom." His conclusions were that the presence of proverbial wisdom in the laws might not be "a late gloss but rather [as] a survival of ancient legal procedure."[16] The implications of these observations for the wisdom tradition in ancient Israel were developed by Audet. Noting several different levels of authority in ancient Israel (family, tribe, city), he theorized that behind the law of the city lies the unwritten law of the family or clan. Indeed, the authority of such urban law depends upon the authority structure of the family. Audet then turned his attention to wisdom and its origins. Rejecting both theses dependent on a borrowing from ancient Near Eastern models and, also, the notion of a general (popular) reflection process, he set forth the proposition that wisdom is *paideia,* an educational process that developed in the primitive body of the family. He concluded his short study by equating the functions of wisdom and law in early tribal settings. It was only with the growing complexity of society and its different institutions that law and wisdom became differentiated and ultimately placed in separate literary traditions.[17]

Gerstenberger further develops this line of thinking with a full-scale evaluation of the prohibition in the legal sections of the Old Testament.[18] After a thorough study of the occurrences and formal characteristics of the prohibition in the legal materials, he turns to the question of its origin and suggests that the clan *(Sippenethos)* provides the necessary setting. The prohibition is the authoritative command of the clan or family and it is reflective of and dependent upon a sacred order of life. To illustrate and verify this suggestion he turns first to texts such as Jer. 35 and Lev. 18, in order to demonstrate both the authority structure of the family and the type of legal regulations which governed that group. Gerstenberger then examines the wisdom literature itself and finds enlightening parallels in form and content between legal prohibitions and wisdom admonitions, especially in Prov. 22–24. Ultimately this study confirms, with important detailed analyses, the position of Audet. The study of Richter also confirms the formal analysis of Gerstenberger, but suggests another, later, setting for the origins of the wisdom admonitions, namely the school.[19] It should be noted that subsequent studies by Murphy, Crenshaw, and others have accepted the ethos of the tribe or family as one important locus for the origins of wisdom without necessarily rejecting the notion that the monarchy was another such locus.

In summary, the suggestion of a clan or tribal ethos as the specific setting for the beginning of the wisdom tradition in pre-monarchical Israel must be taken seriously. Not only are the form-critical observations upon which this thesis is based strong ones, but the setting proposed is compatible with the thesis of popular or folk wisdom as well. The parallels drawn by Gemser demonstrate the possibility that proverbial material not only could function to provide timeless aphorisms, but had important social functions as well. Thus, for example, the assertion by Lindars that Jotham's fable is a social commentary is strengthened and given a more understandable context if a society with overlapping authority structures as suggested by Audet is accepted. Moreover, the role of the elders as potential fabricators, adjudicators, and transmitters of wisdom as *paideia* is also strengthened, though our evidence for this phenomenon remains oblique.

To be sure, the characteristics of pre-monarchical wisdom are not greatly clarified by the existence of a clan ethos standing behind it. But, once more, the evidence of popular and clan wisdom in this period indicates a much more general function than we have been accustomed to suggest for later periods. If the development of wisdom is more difficult to trace as a result, its interconnections with other traditions in early Israel are easier to explain.

This chapter has been more concerned with the genesis of the wisdom tradition in ancient Israel before the monarchy than with the interrelationship of wisdom and other traditions which will be the focal point of this study in subsequent chapters. It is significant, however, that the texts which provide the basis for this evaluation of the beginnings of Israelite wisdom are found in non-wisdom literature! To be sure, there are a number of sayings in Proverbs which are important in discussing the nature of early wisdom, but most of these become significant only when compared and contrasted with the popular sayings and legal materials found elsewhere. At least for the early period, the evidence suggests that wisdom was fully integrated into the societal structures, available to all, capable of and essential to the interrelationship of a number of interests and concerns.

The thesis of a number of scholars that the wisdom of early Israel was transmitted through the Canaanites and other ancient Near Eastern civilizations has not been discussed in this chapter. This is due in part to the lack of textual evidence in Canaanite civilization, and also to the fact that most advocates of this position presuppose the monarchy as the institution responsible for such a development. Nevertheless, the presence of popular wisdom in Canaanite city-states is difficult to deny, regardless of the minimal evidence. There is no reason to believe that many of the non-Yahwistic sayings did not have their origin in this milieu, though the precise provenance is difficult to pinpoint. What can be maintained, however, is that a clan or tribal ethos provides the best explanation for the setting and transmitting of the pre-monarchical wisdom traditions found in the Old Testament. A dichotomy between the teachings and functions of that wisdom and the religious orientation of the Canaanite civilizations does not appear to exist in any significant way in this period.

Although our sources for this brief examination of wisdom in the pre-monarchical period have been found primarily in non-wisdom literature, the question of wisdom influence is not raised in any important way. There are two reasons for this. First, our knowledge of the wisdom tradition itself is simply too amorphous to posit influence. Surely the critics are correct when they state that to define influence presupposes one can identify with some clarity the source of the influence. A corollary to this observation and the second reason is the nature of the textual evidence itself. The material is too disparate and our ability to date the material too imprecise to draw large-scale conclusions. The most that can be said regarding wisdom, its interaction with and potential influence on other traditions in pre-monarchical Israel, is that wisdom was present in a variety of forms and concerns and that it was utilized in a number of ways by later authors of non-wisdom literature.

The significance of this chapter for our further investigation of wisdom and tradition lies in the implications for constructing a picture of Israelite society at that time. The distinctions often made between wisdom and other functional tasks of a society, as epitomized in the literature produced, do not seem to be valid, for this period at least. Wisdom and law, wisdom and authority, whether secular or religious, cannot be separated. Moreover, the particular genres usually associated with wisdom are often utilized in a number of different ways to make social and theological commentary on diverse aspects of societal life. Thus the wisdom tradition in pre-monarchical Israel may be seen to provide the loci for special concerns ultimately expressed in a variety of different literary forms and at the same time wholly integrated into a society composed of many such loci. As Israelite society becomes more complex and more differentiated, the wisdom tradition may be expected to become, on the one hand, more identifiable as a separate phenomenon and, on the other hand, more capable of influencing and interacting with other traditions in society. Surely the institution of the monarchy in Israel provides the impetus for such a development and it is to this phenomenon we now turn.

CHAPTER III
WISDOM IN THE EARLY MONARCHY

Until the recent focus on the clan/family as a possible origin for Israelite wisdom, the beginnings of the wisdom tradition were usually assigned to the period of the early monarchy. Literary and sociological parallels from Egypt and Mesopotamia and the attribution of much of the wisdom literature to Solomon made the categorization "royal wisdom" an easy and logical one. In this chapter we will focus on the non-wisdom literature of the early monarchical period which, according to a number of scholars, contains wisdom vocabulary, motifs, and theology. After examining the texts which illustrate these claims we will synthesize the conclusions made in an effort to determine the nature of the wisdom tradition in this period.

Analysis of the early monarchical texts is difficult not only because of the methodological issues and dangers we have already noted, but also because the resolution of source-critical problems and the relationship between these texts is far from certain. The scholarly consensus regarding authorship and date will be followed with significant alternatives recognized when necessary. Another problem which arises is the interrelationship of scholarly arguments. For example, the claim that a particular text reflects a connection with the wisdom tradition is often buttressed by the acceptance of similar claims for other texts. The validity of such argumentation can only be evaluated after all the evidence has been examined. Thus we will focus our attention on the particular texts first, reserving judgment about their interconnection and potential significance until the initial examination is completed.

The Yahwist

Genesis 2–3. Many scholars have found evidence of the wisdom tradition in Gen. 2–3. The most thorough recent analysis of the text from this perspective remains that of Alonso-Schökel, who is dependent on the work of Dubarle for his starting point.[1] The purpose of Genesis 2–3, according to Alonso-Schökel and Dubarle, is to account for the "human condition" which provides the explanation for the fall and the key to understanding the future history of man and Israel. The narrative is faithful to the mentality of the sages by moving downward, or inductively, from father to son. Thus the Yahwist begins with his own experience and attempts to relate this to the origins of man.[2] Wisdom is also found in the use of four sapiential motifs: the knowledge of good and evil; the shrewdness (*ᶜarum*) of the serpent; the sage, that is, Adam; and the detailed discussion of the four rivers. All of these are related to similar concerns in the wisdom literature itself, although no attempt to find contemporary parallels (and therefore direct influence) is made. The stylistic dexterity of Genesis 2–3 and the occurrence of similar literary conventions in wisdom literature is noted. Finally, Alonso-Schökel attempts to reconstruct the thought process of the writer, "familiar with the sapiential milieu" which resulted in the narrative. Subsequent studies have found further evidence of the wisdom tradition in the vocabulary *(ḥamad, hiškil)* and other motifs (the serpent's advice leading to death; inordinate desire; the curses upon the land [thorns] and man [frustrating work]) which have parallels in wisdom literature.[3] Yet, as Alonso-Schökel himself has pointed out, many of the characteristic elements he has labeled as sapiential are common to other traditions as well, most notably those associated with the Deuteronomic movement (e.g., retribution).[4] Perhaps, therefore, our conclusions should be similar to those of Mendenhall, who sees Genesis 3 as a *mašal* dating from the exilic period.[5] This would allow both sapiential and Deuteronomic influence and also be compatible with some current, if not majority, views about the Yahwist.[6]

The fundamental issue raised by maintaining the presence of the wisdom tradition in Gen. 2–3 and attributing this passage to the Yahwist in the early monarchy is *not* the seeming evidence/influence of the wisdom tradition itself or the text's compatibility with wisdom literature. This is usually accepted by most scholars. Rather, the issue is the relationship of the wisdom tradition to creation theology, especially when that theology is perceived to be subordinate to a history of redemption which governs the theology of the Yahwist. Both the role of creation in Israelite theology and the development of wisdom from "secular" to "religious" to "theological" are at stake here.[7] While there can be no doubt that for the Yahwist the notion of redemptive history is central, the focus on human capability and responsibility is not only present here, but other passages attributable or closely related to the Yahwist have this focus as well (e.g., the Joseph Story). Without maintaining that the author(s) of Genesis 2–3 was a sage, the evidence cited seems to justify the conclusion that the wisdom tradition is present. To assign this text to the Yahwist does not depend on whether redemptive history is the central and primary intention of the author. Rather, it depends on the assertion that creation theology as developed in the wisdom tradition with its focus on responsibility is (1) not incompatible with such a focus, and (2) not necessarily subordinate, but perhaps even an important part of the Yahwist's overall message.[8] The implications of such a position are broad, and will be discussed below.

Genesis 4–11. While some discussions of Gen. 4–11 have brought out parallels between these chapters and other "wisdom-influenced" texts, establishing "wisdom by association" perhaps, Brueggemann and Whybray have also attempted to find wisdom influence here.[9] Brueggemann has found and traced an emphasis on human responsibility and confidence in the order of life epitomized in wisdom teaching. The use of several wisdom motifs and idioms, centering on the results of being wise and righteous or foolish and wicked constitute his primary parallels, with many proverbial passages cited. Whybray finds evidence for the wisdom tradition only in the Tower of Babel story, which he perceives to be a kind of parable and related to Gen. 3. Overall (unlike Gen. 2–3), while parallels to proverbial teaching cannot be overlooked, the textual evidence seems only to indicate compatibility with the wisdom literature and not necessarily a dependence on the tradition associated with it. Still, such compatibility may indeed reflect a social and theological picture of the early monarchy which forces us to recognize that an overcompartmentalization of wisdom and other traditions has occurred.

Exodus 1:8–2:10. The narrative of the birth of Moses has been tentatively classified as a "historicized wisdom tale" by Childs.[10] The significance of this proposal, and those concerning the Joseph Story and Succession Narrative, is that the *entire passage* under consideration is perceived to be transmitted by the wisdom tradition. While such proposals do not maintain that this is wisdom literature, they do have important implications for the relationship of wisdom to the Yahwist, for example, as well as for the necessary (if undefined) sociological base presupposed. After the later traditions and redactional perspectives have been recognized in the birth narrative, the following evidence for location and transmission of this story within the wisdom tradition are given: vocabulary; the stereotyping and polarizing of characters (Pharaoh, the midwives); the presence of "fear of God"; the role of counselor; and parallel concerns and emphases with the Joseph Story, also seen to be a historicized wisdom tale and attributed to the Yahwist. Recognition of this passage as influenced and transmitted by the wisdom tradition depends partially on other hypotheses concerning the Joseph Story and the nature of wisdom in the early monarchy. Nevertheless, Childs has made a cogent and non-dogmatic case which must be added to others.

The Joseph Story, Genesis 37–50. Any discussion of the interrelationship between Israel's wisdom tradition and the Joseph Story must start with the thesis of von Rad.[11] Von Rad began with four presuppositions and observations: (1) that the Joseph Story is different from what preceded, that it had its own internal integrity and could be viewed as an independent whole; (2) that the Joseph Story was best designated as a novella, a short story with a particular purpose, as is the Succession Narrative; (3) that the Joseph Story was a product of the Solomonic Enlightenment, a period characterized by a strong emphasis on man (the "anthropological factor") and his education, the purpose of the wisdom movement; and finally, (4) that wisdom in the early monarchy was royal wisdom, connected to the court. This wisdom played an important role in the enlightenment and had as one of its main purposes the educating of administrators. Von Rad saw Joseph as a paradigm of the ideal administrator and the story as a whole the product of wisdom. This story has a didactic intention garbed in wisdom theology, to demonstrate how to become a good administrator. Many of the attributes which Joseph possessed (the fear of Yahweh; patience, prudence; etc.) were related to sentences with similar concerns in Proverbs. Theological teachings about the relationship between man and God, the way God's purposes are worked out, were also seen to be the same. Finally, the fact that the Joseph Story has no historico-political interests, no emphasis on the cult, no *Heilsgeschichte,* and the supposition of Egyptian influence and parallels cemented the conclusions von Rad reached.

That von Rad wrote this study before the wave of "wisdom influence" scholarship occurred and that his conclusions were compatible with theories about the nature of wisdom derived from wisdom literature alone helped make this interpretation important. Recently, however, the view that the Joseph Story is a wisdom novella has come under attack not simply from those who raise methodological questions but also, and perhaps more importantly, from those who have devoted serious study to the Joseph Story itself.[12] Coats, for example, has not dismissed the wisdom elements found in the story. But on the basis of other non-wisdom concerns and characteristics and the function of the story as a whole, he has rejected the generic description of wisdom novella and the provenance of royal wisdom, if not the court. Both Coats and Whybray have called for a serious reevaluation of traditional source-critical theories about the Joseph Story (JE) in light of the conclusions, put forth by von Rad and affirmed by them, of a single author for the majority of these chapters.[13] Whybray has, on the basis of further study of vocabulary, remained closer to von Rad's original position than Coats.[14] Coats has argued for a generic similarity between Gen. 39–41, the section of the Joseph Story dealing with Joseph's skill and wisdom, and the dream narrative of Solomon (1 Kings 3:5-28). Both of these passages reflect much wisdom teaching, demonstrating how to use power, and can be considered political legends. Ultimately we must agree with the more conservative positions and conclude that the Joseph Story *as a whole* is in all probability *not* a product of the wisdom tradition. Nevertheless, the story manifests definite teachings and ideals which reflect a provenance connected to that of the wisdom tradition and also associated with the court and early monarchy. The Joseph Story is, therefore, a text which contains definite wisdom influence and as such is an important part of the evidence for the wisdom tradition in early Israel. Whether the author of the Joseph Story is the Yahwist or another in the court, the story is to be related to this period (David and Solomon).

Davidic-Solomonic Traditions

The Succession Narrative, 2 Samuel 9–20, 1 Kings 1–2. With the exception of the popular wisdom dealt with above, there is little scholarly discussion of the wisdom tradition in the Davidic and Solomonic traditions before the Succession Narrative.[15] The most thorough analysis of the wisdom tradition and the Succession Narrative is that of Whybray.[16] Accepting von Rad's belief that this story is, like the Joseph Story, a document produced by writers of the Solomonic Enlightenment and perhaps influenced by generically similar Egyptian literature, Whybray puts forth the claim that the Succession Narrative is a dramatization of proverbial wisdom. It is intended by its authors "to teach the doctrines of the wisdom schools."[17] Whybray marshals a great deal of evidence to support his claims. Similarities between the Succession Narrative and Proverbs include: the importance of counsel (ʿeṣah), retribution, Yahweh as the controller of human destiny, and attitude toward the cult. In addition to the citation of much wisdom vocabulary, Whybray notes the use of common forms (simile, comparison) and themes in proverbial literature which have been dramatized in the Succession Narrative (wisdom and folly, the education of children, and the king). The author of the narrative was not simply familiar with proverbial teaching, but was himself a wisdom teacher. Whybray is dependent on von Rad not only for the context of the Succession Narrative, the Solomonic Enlightenment, but also for the parallels he makes with the Joseph Story and the resultant ability to weigh his arguments for the existence of such literature from the wise more heavily. In further study Whybray has again emphasized the presence of the wisdom tradition in the narrative by means of vocabulary and at the same time has seriously questioned some of his earlier presuppositions about the class and institutions implied by such a tradition.[18]

Brueggemann has also found evidence of wisdom teaching in the Succession Narrative.[19] Like Whybray, he assumes a Solomonic Enlightenment and he emphasizes the humanistic and secular orientation of the narrative. He stresses the focus on the non-revelatory nature of God, the "trustedness" and responsibility of man, the "anthropological factor" of von Rad. It should, therefore, not be surprising that Brueggemann and Blenkinsopp find similarities of structure and concern between the Succession Narrative, the Joseph Story, and the prehistory of the Yahwist (Gen. 1–11). Others have questioned the grouping of these texts together (including von Rad!) and their interrelationship will be evaluated below.

Although the Succession Narrative reflects a connection with the wisdom tradition, mere chronological congruence does not justify a close relationship with other literature. Moreover, the interconnections noted by all commentators between the Succession Narrative and redemptive history, as well as other political and theological concerns, make it difficult to consider this text a product of the wisdom tradition alone, reflecting primarily didactic intentions. As in the case of the Joseph Story, it seems possible and the better part of discretion to recognize wisdom influence and yet to maintain an authorship influenced by other traditions and concerns as well. The other alternatives either dilute the notion of a wisdom tradition, maintaining that its idiom and influence is so readily accessible that it can no longer be considered to have any sociological and historical particularity, *or* they posit a wisdom tradition based primarily on the model of Egypt, for which there is little evidence in Old Testament history.

1 Kings 3–11. Virtually all commentators find evidence for the wisdom tradition in these chapters. Whybray, Alt, Scott, and Coats, to name but a few, have found wisdom here.[20] The types of wisdom reflected in Solomon's teaching, vocabulary, the wisdom legend in 1 Kings 3, the literary nature of the passage and possible Egyptian parallels are among the reasons cited. The real question raised by an evaluation of this material is its date. Is it, for example, the *basis* of the later attributions of wisdom to Solomon found in Proverbs and Qoheleth? Or, is it the subsequent *result* of such proverbial wisdom collections needing a royal figure (note the Egyptian parallels) to provide authority? Although Scott has argued cogently for the latter alternative, it is difficult to dismiss all of the evidence cited as late. It is likely that Solomon established monarchical structures, with appropriate personnel, based at least partially on Egyptian models. It is also probable that a part of the ideology which provided the *raison d'etre* of his reign is to be found in legends stressing his wisdom, particularly if specific literary forms are associated with him. This view is strengthened in the light of similar legends about Joseph and David reflecting wisdom influence and provenance, for surely this would have been an important concern for any royal wisdom. In spite of the attempts of Alt and others to define more fully the nature of the wisdom possessed by Solomon, the text itself seems only to reflect that he possessed it. This is itself a clue to the nature, if not the contents, of the wisdom tradition.

The Song of Moses: Deuteronomy 32. A number of scholars have found wisdom influence in the Song of Moses.[21] The opening formula, often considered part of a covenantal lawsuit form, has also been characterized as "invocation of the teacher" and parallels to the double appeal to heavens and earth have been found in other poetry and ancient Near Eastern wisdom. The association of corruption with lack of understanding and several linguistic affinities (vocabulary) are also cited as evidence. Whether or not the song is to be dated in the early monarchy is much debated, but it does reflect a period when many pentateuchal traditions have already been melded together, perhaps during the time of the Deuteronomic reform. In any case, the theological emphases in this poem point overwhelmingly to the redemptive history of Israel. In view of this, regardless of a potential contact between Deuteronomy 32 and the wisdom tradition, this poem can be used safely only to reflect a milieu in which wisdom and other traditions freely borrowed and utilized terminology and theological perspectives from each other. However, it cannot aid us in further defining the nature of the tradition itself.[22]

Clan Wisdom

It is in the period of the early monarchy or perhaps prior to it that the cult adapted the precepts of the clan which were expressed in a "father-son" dichotomy. These precepts became laws, according to the proponents of the theory. Whybray has seriously questioned this theory because of the insignificant occurrences of *hokmah* and other characteristic wisdom terminology in these laws.[23] Although it seems possible that the present purpose and nature of such laws would exclude part of their original rationale, it must be admitted that the laws cited by Gerstenberger and others are not particularly strong evidence for the existence of such wisdom in this period. Since Wolff and others have argued convincingly for the existence of clan wisdom in later periods it seems unwarranted to deny such a phenomenon in the monarchy. Nevertheless, perhaps because of the nature of this tradition, we are unable to find firm textual evidence which might reflect its shape and form. This simply points to the fact that most discussions of clan wisdom do not focus on theological perspectives and message, but rather on the forms which were used to convey the message. Unfortunately, we are unable to provide a clear *Sitz im Leben* for these forms which would win scholarly consensus.

The Wisdom Tradition in the Early Monarchy: Synthesis and Conclusions

The witnesses of the wisdom tradition in non-wisdom texts dating from the early monarchy have provided a great number of characteristics and concerns. All of these texts contain other traditions as well, so the first conclusion which may be reached is that the wisdom tradition is from the beginning an integral, inseparable part of Israel's self expression and theological witness in the Old Testament. The wisdom tradition has been concerned to express itself in the traditional "two ways" theology, manifesting this in several implicit or explicit polarities (wise-foolish, just-unjust, etc.) and the retributional schema which accompanies such polarities. Wisdom theology has often been said to be creation theology, and evidence of this has been suggested from an early period. Wisdom emphasizes the capabilities, responsibilities, the "trustedness" of man. Wisdom focuses on experiential data which can be analyzed and evaluated, stressing not the authority of God through direct revelation but rather emphasizing the hidden yet sure nature of Yahweh as establisher and controller of man. Wisdom has been concerned to speak of leadership in administrative positions and the skills necessary to maintain it. The monarchy has also been an important institution for the wisdom tradition and the legitimation of Solomon, as David's rightful successor and as embued with God-given gifts of insight necessary for a successful reign, has received much attention. These concerns have been expressed in a variety of ways: stereotypical figures, proverbial teachings, distinctive vocabulary, and the use of myth and legend, among others. In almost all cases, the wisdom literature itself, especially Proverbs, has been appealed to as the source of the literary patterns and theological emphases found in the texts studied, or at least, a compatible reflection of the nature of the wisdom tradition of this period.

And yet, if the evidence for the wisdom tradition in the early monarchy is merely catalogued and collated, we are left with a picture which not only is unhelpful in determining the nature and scope of this tradition, it is manifestly unfair to the texts from which the evidence is taken. Compatibility with Proverbs is not enough, for the literary forms and teachings in this book are themselves diverse and subject to many different interpretations regarding

theological development, social provenance, etc. More importantly, the Joseph Story and Succession Narrative, to cite just two
examples, represent the combination of quite different traditions,
having different purposes and intentions. It is, therefore, necessary
to differentiate the evidence for the wisdom tradition in these texts.
Then, hopefully, not only will clarity be provided, but also the
nuancing of the nature, scope, and concerns of the wisdom tradition
itself will be made possible.

While many elements common to all characterizations of
wisdom in whatever period (confidence in experience, two-ways
theology, etc.) can be found in our texts, when viewed together
there are fundamental differences as well. The emphasis on the
knowledge of good and evil and its connection to creation is to be
found only in Genesis 2-3. While other texts may presuppose such a
framework, only this text focuses on what is often considered to be a
"later" development in wisdom theology. The combination of this
emphasis with mythical motifs is also unique to this text. Over
against Gen. 2-3 the four other texts share one point in common:
they utilize and develop their teaching around legendary material
(Joseph, Moses, David, Solomon). Regardless of their differences,
this observation strengthens the role for the wisdom tradition in the
transmission and use of these legends to illustrate particular
teachings. Yet the type and place of each legendary figure are quite
different, reflecting a concern or ability of the wisdom tradition to
embrace many aspects of Israelite culture at one and the same time.
The wisdom elements in the Joseph Story are concerned with the
administrator, the assistant to the king, often seen to be the
paradigm of the "wise man" in the early monarchy. The birth
narrative of Moses, on the other hand, is meant to provide further
legitimation and therefore authority to a figure usually associated
with the cult. The close connection between cult and monarchy
often made on other grounds is further confirmed by this text, with
the wisdom tradition concerned to aid in the underpinning and
legitimation of both institutions.

The Succession Narrative, composed of many legends concerning David and his family, reflects a concern to legitimate the successor of David, namely Solomon. The Solomonic traditions in 1 Kings 3-11 reflect much of the same intention, except that the focus is now on Solomon alone, on his wisdom, requested of and given by God. Although there are significantly different uses of wisdom in these two texts,[24] in both the wisdom tradition has been found influential in the utilization of monarchical legends to legitimate and give authority to some aspect of the monarchy. But to legitimate the succession of a king by stressing the hidden but sure way of God in the process is surely not the same as legitimation of a *particular* king by calling attention to his skills and wisdom. In many ways, then, although the figure of Solomon is central to both texts, the intentions behind each story point to a different use, and perhaps even a different source, of the wisdom tradition.

The following picture of the wisdom tradition and its provenance emerges from the various contexts studied.

Monarchical Institutions	*Clan Wisdom*
Genesis 2-3 (4-11) Joseph Story	
Succession Narrative	
Solomon's Wisdom	
Moses Birth Narrative	
(Deuteronomy 32: Song of Moses?)	

At least three different authors or schools are represented by these texts (J, Succession Narrative, 1 Kings 3—11). In addition, all of them manifest some later redactional perspectives as well. The common ground is not Yahwistic theology or similar usage of wisdom forms, themes, and theology, but rather an association with the institutions of the monarchy. Although Brueggemann and Blenkinsopp have traced similar themes and structures in Gen. 1–11, the Joseph Story, and the Succession Narrative, the different purposes for which they were written and their individual integrity and cohesiveness make it improbable that such similarities reflect common authorship. More important, the different functions represented by the legends and myths behind the present texts make it difficult to assume that the wisdom tradition was perceived by these texts in the same way. This is not to deny a certain similarity of theological perspective. But it was utilized in quite different ways, not simply by J or the author of the Succession Narrative, but also by the wisdom tradition itself.

On the basis of the non-wisdom traditions of this period, what, then, does the wisdom tradition look like in the monarchy? First, it is thoroughly tied to the institutions of the monarchy, found often in texts which have as their function the legitimation of these institutions. Second, the wisdom tradition may be in part responsible for the transmission of legends and myths often used for legitimation. Therefore, the wisdom tradition may be a source for other monarchical writers who add to and nuance these legends with different concerns and theological perspectives. Third, there are at least two different uses of the wisdom tradition: first, as a source and means of legitimation; second, as a theological perspective and emphasis which stresses the framework for man's ability and responsibility. It does not seem necessary to posit two different forms, perhaps with different settings, for these dissimilar though compatible functions of the wisdom tradition. Rather, it seems best to recognize *both* in one wisdom tradition and attribute the different uses to the authors who controlled the non-wisdom texts in which they are found. Finally, regarding the social class and setting of such a tradition, there appears to be some evidence that the administrators of the monarchy were at least a part of its constituency. While the question of wisdom schools cannot be answered definitively, it is difficult to attribute the traditions in Gen. 2-3 and 1 Kings 3-11 to administrators with no responsibility for the transmission of wisdom teaching. As a result, the hypothesis that places of training which might not simply deal with the practical wisdom of bureaucracy but also be concerned with the theological underpinning of such wisdom is an attractive one.[25]

It is important to stress that virtually all those who discuss the wisdom tradition of this period are in one way or another influenced by the parallel phenomena in Egypt. Thus schools, administrators, the king himself, and scribes are all based on Egyptian models. More importantly, the Joseph Story, the Succession Narrative, and 1 Kings 3-11 are compared to similar Egyptian literature. While the wisdom tradition in Israel is distinctively Israelite in many ways, we cannot overemphasize the importance Egyptian wisdom has had in defining its nature and scope.[26]

How dependent is such a picture of the wisdom tradition on the thesis of a Solomonic Enlightenment? Does the tradition itself confirm it? The proliferation of literary works commonly attributed to the early monarchy makes such a thesis attractive, with or without a wisdom tradition. What seems at issue is not, therefore, the literary creations of this period, but rather their character, context, and intention, and hence the appropriateness of the designation "enlightenment." Von Rad has argued that the nature of this enlightenment involved a transition from pan-sacral to secular as witnessed by the Joseph Story, the Yahwist, etc. However, if Gen. 2-3 actually reflects the presence and use of wisdom creation theology, albeit not as developed as in later wisdom literature, then the development from secular to theological which von Rad assigns to a later period has already begun by the time of the early monarchy! If, then, "enlightenment" is intended to refer to a growing awareness of the secular dimensions of Israel and not simply the creative use and literary formulation of epics and narratives which reflect far more than simply this, then the term is indeed a misnomer. On the other hand, the term can simply pinpoint an important period in the growth and development of various theological and historical traditions. Then, regardless of the fact that we may disagree about the nature of the traditions and their contributions to such a development, the existence of such an enlightenment is difficult to deny.[27]

How does such a picture of the wisdom tradition relate to theories developed from the wisdom literature alone? First, no textual material in the Old Testament, wisdom or non-wisdom, enables us to see clearly the precise setting and class associated with the tradition, though the recent studies of Kovacs are compatible with the witness of non-wisdom literature.[28] Second, one of the basic characteristics of wisdom in this period has been its secular nature, its concern with non-theological issues and problems in Israelite society. Surely the parallels found especially in the Joseph Story and the Succession Narrative confirm this as one major characteristic of the tradition in this period. We find it difficult to accept the hypothesis of McKane that such wisdom was non-Yahwistic, non-theological, however.[29] Although the legends transmitted by the wisdom tradition may be easily separated from their Yahwistic context, this is less easily done with vocabulary and theological emphases. Moreover, the presence of the wisdom tradition in a variety of theological writings makes it difficult to believe this could have occurred if the tradition itself perceived its teachings as separable from more explicitly theological ones.

We must also disagree with von Rad, Fox, McKane, and a host of other commentators who, basing their conclusions about wisdom's development primarily on the wisdom literature itself, assert that "theological" wisdom (creation, etc.) is a late development. While we cannot attribute the creation narrative to wisdom writers, the presence of wisdom used theologically in connection with a creation doctrine seems difficult to deny. Thus perhaps the conclusions of Bauer-Kayatz and others who argue for an early dating for Proverbs 1-9 must be given more credence.[30] We are not arguing, however, for a dependence of this theological wisdom or the "secular-anthropological" wisdom of the Joseph Story and Succession Narrative upon specific passages in Proverbs. Rather, the diversity of the perspectives represented in Proverbs would appear to have been too neatly placed into a developmental pattern which presupposes the wisdom tradition became theological only in a later period, in response to a variety of "Yahwistic" influences. Such a theory of development will not explain Gen. 2-3

or the other texts studied which manifest direct connections with J
and many different institutions associated with the monarchy under
the umbrella of Yahwism.

Finally, a word should be said about the wisdom tradition's
interrelationship with other traditions of the period. It is interesting
that while *all* of the texts we have examined are traditionally located
in Judah and more specifically, Jerusalem, only 1 Kings 3-11 focuses
on the Davidic covenant traditions. The Moses birth narrative is to
be connected with the Exodus-Sinai complex rather than the
patriarchal-promise tradition often connected to the Davidic
covenant. Thus the wisdom tradition is to be related to two major
streams of tradition in the history of Israel, the David-Zion and
Exodus-Sinai traditions. This, on the one hand, confirms the
hypothesis of Cross and others regarding the connection of these
two complexes in Judah. On the other hand, it witnesses to the
importance of the wisdom tradition in expressing fundamental
theological perspectives pertinent to many different constituencies
in ancient Israel.

But how is the wisdom tradition to be separated from others?
Where does its uniqueness lie? Do we, finally, have to admit that
Whybray is right, that it is no more than a tradition of intellectuals?
Or to affirm with Heaton that "the 'Wisdom' tradition of the Old
Testament is no more and no less than the 'classical' tradition of its
educated men"?[31] Although we have been unable to provide a
clearly defined social matrix for the wisdom tradition in the early
monarchy, the distinctive theological perspectives, vocabulary,
forms, et al., seem to point to more than just an intellectual
tradition. *These* intellectuals are interested in legitimation, in
particular aspects of the monarchy, and their literary contribution
and influence while widespread is not so amorphous or omnipresent
that we are unable to define and distinguish it.

Nevertheless, the claims of Murphy that the wisdom tradition is
an integral and inseparable part of the Israelite world view and
Wirklichkeitverstandnis is surely confirmed by our analysis of early

monarchical texts.[32] Whybray, in asserting the presence of wisdom
elements in the Succession Narrative, finds a tension between
redemptive theology and the wisdom tradition's empirical perspectives in both the Joseph Story and the Succession Narrative.[33] Such
tensions could surely be found in Gen. 2-3, Exod. 1:8f. and 1 Kings
3-11. And yet, perhaps the most important observation of our study
to this point is that such tension, for the authors at least, really
doesn't exist. Surely the texts, by containing both the history of the
Yahwist or similar theologians and the different perspectives of the
wisdom tradition, may be understood by means of such polarities.
But such perspectives destroy the unity and integrity of the texts
themselves, which witness to a conceptualization of God working in
history through men which needs both wisdom and the Yahwist and
cannot choose—wouldn't think of choosing—between them. Such a
situation, not simply for the texts represented but also for the period
as a whole is witnessed to by the existence of so many different uses
and perspectives of wisdom and other traditions in the early
monarchy.

CHAPTER IV
WISDOM AND THE PROPHETS

The pre-exilic prophetic literature is found in the next chronological period where evidence of interaction with the wisdom tradition is to be found. It is interesting to note that, until relatively recently, the prophets were considered to have influenced the (assumed) later wisdom writers. The passages in the prophets which resembled wisdom literature in terms of style, form, vocabulary, or similar theological perspective were thought to be genuinely prophetic in provenance, which the wisdom writers subsequently utilized in their teaching. As one commentator stated: "One has to remember that the underlying purpose of the wisdom writers was to apply the religion of the Law and the Prophets, so far as this had developed, to the practical, every day life of the individual."[1] Such a view was dependent on a still current consensus that the majority of wisdom literature in its present form was to be dated in the post-exilic period. It also depended on the notion that the prophets represented a new phenomenon in Israel, with a theological perspective quite different from that of the cult, the monarchy, and other carriers of Israelite tradition. Both of these premises have broken down in recent studies of the wisdom literature and the prophets, though the relationship between prophecy and wisdom is still difficult to determine.[2] Moreover, in light of the nature of the evidence for the presence of the wisdom tradition in the early monarchy discussed above, it appears extremely unlikely that the relationship between prophets and wise men was totally one-sided.

Another reason why the conclusion that the prophets influenced wisdom was so easily and naturally reached concerns the nature of the evidence itself. In many of the monarchical texts the issue was not really wisdom influence but wisdom ethos or provenance. That is, large textual units were related to wisdom genres not simply because of vocabulary, themes, forms, etc., but also because the subject matter of the *whole unit* was of interest to the wise. This is not the case for prophetic literature. The prophetic books themselves are difficult to divide into large blocks with enough similarity and internal integrity to warrant a generic term. Moreover, the literary passages cited are much smaller in scope, focusing on style, rhetoric, vocabulary, shorter literary forms, theological similarities, et al., which simply are not found throughout the writings of any prophet with consistent and significant frequency. Thus the idea that the wisdom tradition could be responsible for a block of material, such as the Succession Narrative or the Joseph Story, is not probable or even suggested. More important, while in monarchical texts there are suggestions that the wisdom tradition might have been in some way responsible for the literature itself, for the most part there is no such assumption in prophetic literature. A focus on the creativity and individual character of each prophet is partially responsible for such a view.

Because of the character of wisdom influence found and the nature of the prophets themselves, few scholars have attempted to see the prophets as "wise men."[3] Rather, for those who claim wisdom influence in their writings, the prophets are envisioned as borrowing, intentionally or not, directly or indirectly, certain forms, vocabulary, and theology from the wise, to whom many of them also refer directly. There are, as one might guess a number of serious methodological critiques of those who find wisdom influence in the prophets. In the following search for evidence of the wisdom tradition in the prophets we will cite the arguments and evidence given which seem potentially cogent and reasonable, and also pay attention to both the quantity and quality (types) of the parallels cited. The implications of the wisdom influence cited will be evaluated for each prophet, and for the prophets as a whole. Finally, the implications for the shape of the wisdom tradition in this period must be correlated with the conclusions reached about the wisdom tradition in the monarchy in the hopes that a picture of the development of this tradition will emerge. Six pre-exilic prophets will be examined in this chapter: Amos, Hosea, Micah, Isaiah (1-39), Jeremiah, and Habakkuk. Any examination of prophetic literature must be aware of possible later intrusions, even made by wisdom writers themselves. Too often, however, the assumption that wisdom was "late" made such conclusions automatic. In addition, we must be sensitive to the possibility that the *prophets* influenced the wisdom tradition by means of forms, vocabulary, and theology. The possibility that such influence was brought about by a prophetic reinterpretation of contemporary wisdom teaching, itself an influence on the prophets, must be considered seriously.[4]

Finally, a few general thoughts about prophets and wisdom are in order. The prophets do represent a new phenomenon in Israelite religion, regardless of the earlier traditions which they use and upon which they are dependent. Perhaps too much has been made of the distinction between prophetic "word" (*dabar*) and wisdom "counsel" (ᶜesah), which has been nuanced if not created by contemporary epistemological polarities. Nevertheless, a distinction is to be made, and the issue is primarily one of authority.[5] There is no doubt that wisdom and prophecy often substantiate and verify their claims in different, if not incompatible, ways.[6] Nevertheless, the very presence of wisdom influence in the prophets warns us against making clear and absolute divisions between ᶜesah and *dabar*.

Our study to this point has suggested that at least from the monarchy on, the wisdom tradition is theological, religious, Yahwistic. We may surely expect conflict between the wisdom tradition and the prophets. But, since wisdom has a tendency both to affirm and legitimate the authoritative institutions of the state, conflict should not automatically presuppose different and incompatible theological perspectives. Rather, the issue may revolve around wisdom's loyalty to the monarchy. The fact that the wisdom tradition is important in the formulation of the Yahwist's corpus, which is the basis of much prophetic teaching, may help to explain the use by the prophets of its idioms and theology despite being at times on the opposite side of the fence. We must also not forget the possibility that another kind of wisdom exists, not connected to the monarchy, which might well be used by prophets in their attacks on the state and its institutions.

Amos

Parallel concerns and formal similarities between Amos and the wisdom literature have long been noted. However, for reasons mentioned above, it has most often been assumed that Amos influenced the later wisdom tradition. Prior to form-critical studies of the prophetic material, it was difficult if not impossible to "locate" most prophets in terms of their social milieu. Thus it is understandable that the prophetic message of Amos, with the normative priority given to it, would determine the question of dependence or influence, rather than his background. With the increasing attention given to the setting of individual genres and styles, and resultant traditio-historical studies, much examination of the background and the formative influences upon the prophets has taken place. Thus the observation and conviction of an early commentator that the style, as well as the substance, of Amos's message was to be explained by the circumstances of his environment has now been taken seriously.[7]

The background of Amos has always been seen as somewhat irregular when compared to other prophets. Not only is his home located in the south and his message in the north, but he reflects little knowledge of or concern with the major traditions of the nation of Judah, the city of Jerusalem. Rather he is said to have come from Tekoa (1:1), a small village south of Jerusalem. References to Isaac (7:9, 16) and Beersheva (5:5, 8:14) seem to confirm a provenance in the southern area of Judah. It is, therefore, not surprising that the peculiarities of Amos's style and message are often associated with traditions which are not in the mainstream of Israelite religion. These "mainstream" traditions are usually connected to the institutions which exercised power, the cult and the monarchy. Moreover, the *absence* of knowledge about the clan and its wisdom, of Edom and its wisdom, is crucial in the suppositions about formative influences and the institutions behind them. The knowledge that Amos represents a use of traditions different from those of Jerusalem reinforces the possibility that he was influenced by clan or family wisdom.

The two scholars most responsible for finding wisdom influence in Amos and attempting to define its nature and provenance are Terrien and Wolff.[8] Terrien began his important study by maintaining that a "proper emphasis on the early date of an oral tradition among the wise may reopen the question of the influences which the prophets have received."[9] Thus while not assuming that the literary forms of Proverbs and similar wisdom literature was early, he felt that many of the wisdom elements of Amos could be rightly seen as "influence" by stressing an oral prehistory for wisdom literature. He noted the southern background of the prophet and argued for the possible interrelationship of Tekoa with Berrsheva and Edom.[10] Thus, the worldview of the international wisdom movement was seen to have a possible formative influence on Amos.

Wolff, while focusing on many of the same passages in Amos and certainly presupposing an oral wisdom tradition, comes to quite different conclusions concerning the nature of the wisdom which influenced Amos. He associates Tekoa not with Edom and international wisdom, but rather with the story of the wise woman from Tekoa in 2 Sam. 14:1-20. He argues that clan wisdom is the background for the wisdom elements to be found in Amos. Wolff is dependent upon Gerstenberger and his studies of apodictic law and the woe oracle for this proposed setting.[11] Though much of his formal evidence is dependent on the work of Terrien, his conclusions and their implications for the nature of the wisdom tradition differ quite radically.

Before attempting to assess the implications for the shape of the wisdom tradition in Amos, the wisdom influence cited by Terrien, Wolff, and others should first be examined. The types of wisdom influence found in the prophetic material may be categorized in four different ways: form/style, theme/motif, vocabulary, and direct mention of the wise. A number of passages reflecting either form or style associated with the wisdom tradition have been found in Amos.[12]

Numerical Formulae. "For three transgressions of Damascus, and for four, I will not revoke the punishment . . ." (1:3; cf. also 1:6, 9, 11, 13; 2:1, 4, 6). This type of formula, which takes the form "for X and for X + 1, . . ." occurs in wisdom literature of the Old Testament and the Apocrypha most frequently (e.g., "Under three things the earth trembles, under four it cannot bear up" . . . [Prov. 30:21ff.]). Wolff notes that usually the focus of these formulae is upon social phenomena. This is consonant with the use of these formulae in Amos, where judgments are proclaimed on the basis of social injustice. Amos, however, changes the formula by not citing four different elements as the parallel passages in wisdom do. Usually one or two transgressions are mentioned. The emphatic function of the formula is kept, the enumerative function is lost. For this reason, although the provenance of the form seems to be clearly in the wisdom tradition, it is best to speak of a stylistic influence. The disparity between the form and function of the forms in wisdom and Amos led one student of these numerical sayings to deny that Amos's use constituted an example of the form at all.[13]

Exhortation Speech (Mahnrede). "Seek good and not evil, that you may live, and let it be so—Yahweh be with you—as you say. Hate evil and love good! Enforce justice in the gate! Perhaps Yahweh will be gracious to a remnant of Joseph" (5:14-15; cf. also 4:4f., 5:4-6). Wolff notes especially the antithetical parallelism found in these sayings and points out similar passages in Proverbs (4:4, 9:6, 13:20, et al.). He claims these sayings reflect family/clan instruction in content and form (versus synonymous parallelism, for example). The thesis of Gerstenberger that the clan was responsible for the origin and function of such forms is developed further by Wolff.[14] It is, once more, difficult to see a "form" here, but rather a style which may indeed go back to the clan.

Woe Oracle. "Woe to those who desire the day of the LORD: Why would you have the day of the LORD?" (5:18, cf. 6:1; and also 2:7, 5:7, 6:3-6, 6:13 [by emendation]). Wolff is once more dependent upon the research of Gerstenberger[15] in maintaining that this form is to be associated with wisdom rather than the more traditional curse formulations of the cult. Gerstenberger posits that the origin of this form is the wise man's reflection on the order of the world. More specifically this wisdom is to be associated with the popular ethos, ultimately with the clan. Since the woe is almost never found in wisdom literature, both Gerstenberger and Wolff argue for a parallel form, the counterpart of the woe, namely the blessing, to be evidence for the wisdom origin of the woe. This thesis has been attacked by many who argue against the connection between blessing and woe.[16] While it is conceivable that this form originates in clan wisdom, it is not one of the more convincing arguments for wisdom influence in Amos.

Didactic/Rhetorical Questions. "Do two walk together, unless they have made an appointment? Does the lion roar in the forest, when he has no prey?" (3:3-6, 8; see also 5:25, 6:12). These questions in Amos are all rhetorical in nature. They appeal to common experience as the basis of understanding the obvious answer. The prophet uses them to emphasize some particular point concerning Yahweh's action. Both Wolff and Terrien note that the basis of authority behind such passages is not revelation (word) but rather common experience, and many parallels from Proverbs are cited (8:2, 16:4, 22:2, 29:13, etc.). To be associated with the question form/style are the comparative sayings ("As the shepherd rescues from the mouth of the lion two legs . . . so shall the people of Israel who dwell in Samaria be rescued . . ." [3:12; cf. 5:3]); comparative questions (6:2, 9:7); or the expanded comparison ("Is not the day of the LORD darkness and not light, and gloom, with no brightness in it?" [5:20]). Most of these sayings have an explicitly experiential basis, usually in nature or natural events, for their teaching or main point. The authority of these sayings rests as much on experiential observation as on the revealed word of Yahweh. Comparisons with wisdom literature are also apt, for surely it is there where similar styles and teaching abound. Whether the content or form can be associated with the clan is debatable, but the similarity to wisdom is not.

In addition to these stylistic elements and forms, Amos is also seen to use a great many themes or motifs which are likewise common to the wisdom tradition. Among these are a concern with social injustice (2:6-7, 4:1, 5:11-12, 8:4, 6; cf. Prov. 14:31, 22:22, etc.), where vocabulary parallels are also made with wisdom literature, and an agreement with wisdom that the underworld is completely under Yahweh's influence (9:2; cf. Prov. 15:11, Job 26:6). Both Wolff and Terrien cite the use of *nekoah* in 3:10 as an example of wisdom vocabulary ("They do not know how to do *right*") although Whybray questions the wisdom provenance of this word.[17] *Sod* ("secret" 3:7) and *kesil* ("Orion" 5:8) are also cited as wisdom vocabulary, although the latter passage is often considered secondary by commentators.

What then can be concluded concerning the question of wisdom influence in Amos and the nature of the wisdom tradition utilized by the prophet? First, almost *all* commetators recognize that at least a portion of the evidence cited has some validity and points to a connection of Amos with wisdom. Second, it is significant, in light of the evidence found in other prophets, that the "wise" are never mentioned. This may indeed be because the northern kingdom had no clearly defined group thus designated, but it may also reflect the rural milieu out of which Amos came. If this is the case, it is difficult to assume a direct influence of the wisdom tradition, as described in the previous chapter, upon Amos. One of the problems with such an assumption is the constant reference to Proverbs and other wisdom literature to illustrate the wisdom provenance of some of Amos's literary and thematic concerns, since these books clearly come from monarchical wisdom.[18] In light of the parallels made with the ancient Near East there is no real difficulty if Terrien's thesis of an international wisdom connection is accepted. If *clan wisdom* is seen as the origin of the tradition behind Amos, however, certain presuppositions have to be made. First, that popular or clan wisdom is found in Proverbs. This is usually debated in detail but not in principle. Second, that such clan wisdom is not immediately taken over by monarchical institutions and stylized, but rather that it continues to be an important phenomenon apart from the institutions of the monarchy and indeed may represent and possess forms and concerns as sophisticated as those found in "later" collections.

It is interesting to note that Amos contains no exact literary parallels with Proverbs, for even the numerical formulae have been adapted rather radically. The significance of this observation becomes clearer after all the prophetic literature is examined, but even now it seems to indicate a provenance potentially different from that of Proverbs, though generically related. Our tentative conclusions about the wisdom tradition as witnessed to by Amos are: (1) that it is to be differentiated from that of the monarchy, both by its literary forms and by its geographical location; (2) that the prophet has utilized it in specific, individual ways to illustrate, and even at times to drive home, his points, but that it does not pervade or color the entire message as was the case in some monarchical material—Amos seems to use the idiom of the wisdom tradition; (3) there is no apparent incompatibility, theologically or epistemologically, between the word of Yahweh as perceived by Amos and the earthly wisdom terminology and literary style, heavily influenced by nature and human experience, they are amalgamated in a seemingly effortless manner to express the prophetic word to Israel.

Hosea

It is generally agreed that the prophet Hosea directed his message to the northern kingdom of Israel, and in contrast to Amos, that he also came from the northern kingdom. Therefore, it is especially interesting and noteworthy that significant evidence of the wisdom tradition has been found in the book, for this is the first literary product to be associated with wisdom which has a northern rather than southern provenance. It is, of course, possible that some of the "wisdom influence" cited is later and to be attributed to a southern redactor. Nevertheless, it is difficult to attribute all of the evidence to this source.

Several literary forms or styles found in Hosea have been compared to wisdom literature. Most noteworthy among these are proverbial and comparative sayings.

> Wine and new wine
>   take away the understanding. (4:11)

> For they sow the wind,
>   and they shall reap the whirlwind.
> The standing grain has no heads,
>   it shall yield no meal;
> if it were to yield,
>   aliens would devour it. (8:7)

> Whoever is wise, let him understand these things:
>   whoever is discerning, let him know them;
> for the ways of the LORD are right,
>   and the upright walk in them,
>   but transgressors stumble in them. (14:10[9])[19]

Therefore I am like a moth to Ephraim,
and like dry rot to the house of Judah. (5:12)

Your love is like a morning cloud,
like the dew that goes early away. (6:4b)

Ephraim is like a dove . . . (7:11)

they are like a treacherous bow . . . (7:16)

Samaria's king shall perish,
like a chip on the face of the waters. (10:7)

With the exception of 14:10, usually considered to be a later addition, all of these sayings (cf. also 14:10, 9; 8:9, 13:3) make their point by reference to natural phenomena which all have experienced. In addition, many parallels in both form and content have been noted in Proverbs. The call to priest, the nation of Israel, and the king in 5:1 has been considered by some to be the opening saying of a teacher *(Lehreroffnungsformel)* and to have its provenance in wisdom circles.[20] In addition to the above, the following have also been used to demonstrate the wisdom tradition in Hosea: numerical formula ("After two days he will revive us, on the third day he will raise us up," 6:2); simile ("They are all adulterers, they are like a heated oven . . . ," 7:4); admonition ("Sow for yourselves righteousness, reap the fruit of steadfast love; break up your fallow ground . . . ," 10:12); and reiteration and concantenation (2:23f).

Concerning themes, motifs, and vocabulary, perhaps the most often noted similarity between Hosea and the wisdom literature is the emphasis on the knowledge of God and the use of the verb "to know" (cf. 4:1-3, 6 *[da°at]*; 6:6, 2:22, 5:3, 4, 9, 6:3, 7:9, 8:2, 4, 9:7, 11:3, 13:4, 5, 14:10 *[yada°]*). Most, however, relate this knowledge to the cult, more specificially to priestly torah or instruction (cf. 4:6).[21] While it may be unwarranted to consider Hosea's concern with knowledge as wisdom influence, nevertheless this may be an example of an interface between wisdom, prophecy, and cult which ultimately led to the equation of cultic torah with wisdom. Moreover, the "knowledge of God" cannot be simply equated with cultic instruction, for its use by Hosea has been broadened to include all aspects of individual morality.[22] Other concerns of Hosea connected to the wisdom tradition include: the possible reference to a proverbial teaching concerning boundaries (5:10); the contrast between good and evil (14:3 [2]); the use of the verb "to understand or discern" in 4:14; and the obvious wisdom teaching in 14:10[9]. While several references are made to royal functionaries (5:1, 10; 9:15; 13:10), there is no ostensible reference to the wise or their professional functions and perspectives.

When all of the evidence for the use of, and influence by, the wisdom tradition in Hosea is surveyed, the conclusions to be reached are at best ambiguous. On the one hand, even without Hosea 14:10 there are a number of proverbial sayings, and the use of vocabulary and concepts "at home" in wisdom literature is difficult to deny. On the other hand, many of the parallels noted are inconsequential, probably common to all educated people, and therefore of little help in our quest to trace the wisdom tradition in this period. We cannot agree with Heaton that the evidence "suggests either the existence of a school of wisdom in the northern kingdom at the Court of Samaria, or, possibly, a thorough reediting of his oracles by a scribe of the southern kingdom who shared the prophet's outlook."[23] Surely the Book of Hosea in its present form witnesses to a basic compatibility between its prophetic message and that of a later wisdom writer (i.e., the author of 14:10), but the reason for such compatibility must be searched for elsewhere than the book itself. On the other hand, Hosea's critical attitude toward the cult, shared with many prophets, and the use of many proverbial expressions may point to a basic similarity in perspective. This may, with other evidence, be used to help explain the reasons behind the common call to experiential authority and the development of wisdom. In addition, if the existence of a wisdom tradition lying behind Hosea were to be postulated, it would certainly more closely resemble the tradition to be found in the early monarchy of Judah than that of Amos. The literary forms and perspectives utilized in Hosea do not reflect clan concerns and have more direct parallels with Proverbs than Amos.

Finally, regardless of our capacity to identify and locate the wisdom tradition which Hosea may have used, the presence of these particular forms, styles, themes, motifs, and vocabulary are important in evaluating the overall message of the prophet. While surely dependent upon a belief that Yahweh has judged Israel and yet still proclaiming that God may have mercy, Hosea's attempt to place part of his message into a proverbial idiom with its appeals to common sense and experience is a potentially important model for contemporary preaching and teaching. Moreover, his focus on knowledge and its proper use is a call for serious reexamination of our own use of present cultic traditions.

Micah

It is immediately striking that Micah, like Amos, did not come from Jerusalem but rather Morosheth, a small village in southwestern Judah. Therefore, it is not particularly surprising that the wisdom tradition which is to be found in Micah is "clan wisdom" and that the major proponent of this view is H. W. Wolff.[24] The evidence for a clan wisdom background in Micah is slim in comparison to that of Amos, however. Some of the formal elements Wolff cites are the woe oracle in chapter 2; the lamentation using nature comparisons in 1:8ff.; the juxtaposition of evil and good in 3:2; the concern with bribery in 3:11; the occurrence of yada (to know) and 'eṣah (plan, counsel) in 4:12; and tušiyyah (wisdom) in 6:9 (often considered a later gloss). What is valuable about the study of Micah's background, however, is not whether we are able to identify wisdom forms in the prophet. That, indeed, is questionable. Rather, what is important is the (common) cultural background Wolff suggests for Amos and Micah and the implications this has for more fully explicating the nature of the clan wisdom tradition. Concerns with social injustice (2:2, 3:3) and the antagonism of the prophet towards the leaders of Jerusalem suggest a setting which is quite distinct from and opposed to the urban society of Jerusalem. Though the message of Amos is not directed to Judah, the same concerns permeate his teaching as well. Whether or not we can accept the hypothesis that Micah was a clan elder, we can postulate a setting different from that in which early monarchical wisdom is to be found. Such an observation strengthens the possibility that a clan setting, with its own teachings and, perhaps, special forms, might be responsible for some of the distinct elements in the messages of both Amos and Micah. Once more, the basic difference between clan and monarchical wisdom, as between the wisdom tradition and the cult and prophets, seems not to be a theological one, but rather a sociological one. The different settings engender different teachings and values, though the call to experience, to revelation, the belief in Yahweh, are common to all. The particular message of Micah is impregnated with concern over the wickedness of those in Jerusalem. In this sense, canonically at least, Micah must be taken seriously when evaluating monarchical wisdom and other traditions stemming from that locus.

Isaiah

Virtually all commentators have recognized the presence of wisdom forms, themes, and vocabulary in the teaching of Isaiah of Jerusalem. Some of the so-called wisdom materials are ascribed to later hands, and methodological questions continue to be raised. Nevertheless, the sheer quantity of evidence cited makes it very different not to assume that Isaiah was indeed familiar with the wisdom tradition whose provenance is in biblical wisdom literature. If even a small portion of the evidence cited for the wisdom tradition in the early monarchy is accepted as valid, then such a conclusion about Isaiah and the wisdom tradition is not surprising. In view of the prophet's concern and connection with the monarchy, it would be striking if there were not some knowledge and use of this tradition on his part. Although some of the examples of the wisdom tradition presented have more credence than others, the real debate about wisdom and Isaiah does not revolve around the question of whether there *is* wisdom influence, but rather around the questions of the nature of that wisdom tradition and the prophet's use of it, and the resultant picture of Isaiah. Is, for example, Isaiah to be considered a scribe or sage turned prophet? Is the wisdom tradition attacked by Isaiah antithetical to the prophetic word, thus raising questions of authority and epistemology? Our earlier conclusions about the wisdom tradition in Jerusalem, to which Isaiah is surely related, may aid in answering these and other questions.

It would be impossible to examine all the examples of wisdom in Isaiah cited by scholars. We will deal only with those which are most often discussed, for which strong arguments have been made, and which are most helpful in determining the precise nature of the wisdom tradition in Isaiah and the prophet's use and relationship to it. The first form manifesting potential wisdom influence is found in the opening verses and is labeled as a teacher's opening formula.[25]

> Hear, O heavens, and give ear, O earth;
>   for the LORD has spoken:
> "Sons have I reared and brought up,
>   but they have rebelled against me.
> The ox knows its owner,
>   and the ass its master's crib;
> but Israel does not know,
>   my people does not understand."   (1:2-3)

Comparisons with animals, wisdom vocabulary (to know, to understand), the father-son relationship, and many parallels with similar proverbial passages are cited. It is important to note that, while Löwenclau believes a basic wisdom form is partially responsible for this passage's present structure, the prophet is not simply familiar with wisdom but is correcting it! Isaiah is not beginning with the "fear of God," for example, but rather with the notion of election. "Sons" must know to whom they belong, and this is achieved through a knowledge of God attained by seeing Yahweh's actions in history. While surely the prophet is adding his special concerns and perspective, it is not immediately obvious that the knowledge of Yahweh in "history" *(Heilsgeschichte)* is what is at issue, or that there is a basic incompatibility with wisdom even if this were the case. As noted in our discussion of the Song of Moses (Deut. 32), this and related passages have also been seen as examples of a covenantal lawsuit.[26]

A second form found throughout Isaiah and attributed to wisdom is the woe oracle.

> Woe to those who join house to house,
>   who add field to field,
> until there is no more room,
>   and you are made to dwell alone
>   in the midst of the land . . . (5:8)

> Woe to those who rise early in the morning,
>   that they may run after strong drink,
> who tarry late into the evening
>   till wine inflames them . . . (5:11)

The claim that this form is derived from wisdom is Gerstenberger's, but, as it appears in Isaiah, it has been studied more thoroughly and convincingly by Whedbee.[27] The fact that most of these passages (cf. 5:8-24, 10:1-4, 5, 29:15-16) are characterized by social concerns and imagery parallel to that of Proverbs must be taken seriously. On the other hand, most of the wisdom found in Isaiah is usually associated with the forms and concerns of royal wisdom, different from the clan provenance of the woe oracle. It is possible and probable that at some point the clan wisdom forms found their way into royal wisdom, but the different ethos attributed to these traditions increases the difficulty in ascertaining the relationship between them.

Another form used by Isaiah and attributed to the wisdom tradition is the summary appraisal form.[28]

> This also comes from the LORD of hosts;
> he is wonderful in counsel,
> and excellent in wisdom. (28:29, cf. 14:26-27, 17:14)

The dissimilarity of these forms with other prophets, their non-cultic character, their didactic function, and parallels in wisdom literature (Prov. 1:19, Ps. 49:14[13], Job 8:13, etc.) are among the arguments used for placing this form within the wisdom tradition. There appears to be no antithesis between prophet and wisdom here, rather a common call to authoritative appraisal on the basis of God's wisdom.

Isaiah is also said to have utilized the wisdom form of parable, the most striking and least debatable example being the parable of the farmer.

> Give ear, and hear my voice;
> hearken, and hear my speech.
> Does he who plows for sowing plow continually?
> does he continually open and harrow his ground?
> When he has leveled its surface,
> does he not scatter dill, sow cummin,
> and put in wheat in rows
> and barley in its proper place,
> and spelt as the border?
> For he is instructed aright;
> his God teaches him.
>
> Dill is not threshed with a threshing sledge,
> nor is a cart wheel rolled over cummin;
> but dill is beaten out with a stick,
> and cummin with a rod.
> Does one crush bread grain?
> No, he does not thresh it for ever;
> when he drives his cart wheel over it
> with his horses, he does not crush it.
> This also comes from the LORD of hosts;
> he is wonderful in counsel,
> and excellent in wisdom. (28:23-29; cf. also 1:2-3, 5:1-7)

All of these parables appeal to natural experience and examples to make their point. In every instance the prophet has utilized these forms to proclaim a message not necessarily compatible with that of the wisdom tradition itself. For example, in the parable of the farmer the point seems to be the defense of Yahweh's action as the *prophet,* not the wise man, perceives it (cf. below). It is interesting to note that the clearest examples of this form are not in wisdom literature but rather in non-wisdom traditions (cf., e.g., Nathan's parable above)!

Isaiah also uses, as does Hosea, a number of sayings usually considered proverbial in form and style.

> Turn away from man
> in whose nostrils is breath,
> for of what account is he? (2:22)

> Tell the righteous that it shall be well with them,
> for they shall eat the fruit of their deeds.
> Woe to the wicked! It shall be ill with him,
> for what his hands have done shall be done to him. (3:10-11)

In addition to and in conjunction with these forms, rhetorical questions and comparative sayings are also found. Once more, while nature, human experience, retributional perspectives and the like are found in these passages, they are all utilized to set forth a prophetic message and not to teach wisdom doctrines!

One of the most often-noted wisdom themes or concerns in Isaiah is that of nature and natural knowledge (1:2-3, etc.). While appeals to common experience rather than special revelatory knowledge are certainly characteristic of these passages, perhaps such appeals demonstrate a commonality between prophet and wise man rather than the borrowing of a unique perspective by Isaiah. This observation might also be applicable to the claim that the prophet's concerns with social justice and retributional systems are derived from wisdom. The contrast between God's wisdom and that of man, utilizing much technical wisdom vocabulary, is a far more important observation. Yahweh alone is wise (Isa. 5:19-24, etc.) although his Messiah (11:2ff.) will be given the spirit of wisdom by Yahweh. Throughout Isaiah, this wisdom and counsel of Yahweh is contrasted with those who are wise in their own eyes, be they Israelites or foreigners (3:2-3, 5:21, 8:9-10, 10:5-15, 14:24-27, 19:1-4, 29:13-16, etc.). It is difficult to identify precisely the objects of the prophet's message, though many have associated them with the professional counselors of the king.[29] It is also difficult to assume these attacks represent an ideological confrontation between ʿeṣah and *dabar,* for *both* of these are attributed to Yahweh. What these passages do represent, however, is the conviction that wisdom is to be attributed to Yahweh, that all else is a deception, at least as perceived by this prophet.

One of the most serious attempts to relate Isaiah to the wisdom tradition has focused upon the use of torah by the prophet.[30] In contrast to Hosea, who seems to be dependent upon a cultic conception of torah or instruction, it is claimed that Isaiah is dependent upon a wisdom notion of torah. Yahweh then becomes the imparter of wise instruction,[31] and this is compatible with the use of wisdom and counsel by Isaiah noted above. In order to maintain such a position, certain presuppositions about a prevailing wisdom tradition are necessary. These are compatible with the picture of wisdom found in Chapter III, but also assume institutions of schools and scribal functionaries as well. In view of the many other passages which reflect a wisdom provenance in Isaiah, it is probable that this notion of torah (cf. 1:10, 2:3, 5:24b, 8:16, 20, 30:9) was indeed to be connected with wisdom.

Finally, the use of much vocabulary characteristic of the wisdom tradition must be noted, as well as the explicit mention of offices and groups usually associated with the wise (1:26, 3:1-3, 7:5, 10:1-4, etc.).[32] On the basis of all this evidence it is clear that Isaiah was indeed aware of a tradition which stressed an empirical experiential method of perception, and was, in some sense, influenced by it.

Central to most discussions of Isaiah's use of wisdom is the assumption that the prophet is attacking the wise men in the court of the king. Thus the prophet is using wisdom to correct wisdom! But this is too simplex a way to view the matter, for surely the prophet is

adding his own special perspectives. As a result, we have the flags of
the old dichotomies of reason-revelation, *ʿeṣah-dabar,* nature-history, etc., raised to explain the rationale for such an attack. One
thing is clear: Isaiah believes that *his* perception of what Yahweh is
doing and saying to Israel is the correct one. He attributes to
Yahweh, the source of his perception, precisely those qualities of
knowledge that the "wise" claim for themselves and their positions.
Regardless of his familiarity with the teaching of the wise, it is
difficult to assume, with Fichtner, that Isaiah was a member of the
class of the wise before he became a prophet.[33] Rather, his close
proximity to the court and his literateness (8:1, 16, 30:8) merely
reflects the possibility and indeed, the strong possibility, that he was
familiar with the offices and message of the wisdom tradition. Since
much of his message was directed to the court, it is only natural that
he might utilize its forms, idioms, concepts, and vocabulary in order
to make his message pertinent and, he hoped, effective. The fact
that he uses wisdom forms in an almost effortless way makes it
difficult to accept the assertion that he is totally opposed to the
tradition from which the forms come. Moreover, the fact that
Yahweh is seen to be the source of wisdom need not be perceived as
the introduction of such a conception into the teaching and thought
of the wise. It may be seen, rather, as a reminder, a correction of
thinking which had forgotten its own rationale, its ultimate basis of
authority (contra McKane).

Surely the use of wisdom by Isaiah is an important and positive
aspect of the prophet's message. The attribution of wisdom of
Yahweh is not only an essential foundation for his message to the
wise, but also it provides a foundation for all of his message, for
legitimating the entire proclamation of Isaiah to Jerusalem and
Judah.

The picture of the wisdom tradition found in Isaiah is essentially
a confirmation of points made on the basis of the early monarchical
texts already examined. However, the prophet is warning all of
Judah, including the wise, that too close an association with and too

much reliance upon any institution, in this case the monarchy, is dangerous. *Yahweh,* not the earthly king (cf. 16:1, 5, etc.), is the source of wisdom, and the ultimate legitimator of all. Jensen's thesis that Isaiah's use of torah influenced later wisdom is important here. What is claimed is that wisdom influenced Isaiah and that Isaiah, with his own special notion of wisdom, influenced the later wisdom tradition! Such a picture is difficult to accept if we choose to isolate traditions and/or draw dichotomies which make such interrelationships problematic.

Much more could be said about Isaiah and wisdom, particularly concerning the class/office presupposed by his use of the tradition. This discussion is more easily and appropriately done in connection with the Deuteronomic period and movement, however. There, in addition to a clearer picture of who the wise were, a further and contingent development of the tradition itself can be examined.

Jeremiah

Many connections between Jeremiah and the wisdom tradition in Jerusalem have been made.[34] In light of these claims concerning wisdom and Jeremiah it is interesting that no full scale study of this subject has been done. One reason for this may be the literary complexity of the book, the difficulty in determining precisely which texts can be attributed to Jeremiah, to the Deuteronomic authors, and to later editors or glossators. There has also been a relatively uncritical tendency to characterize certain "wisdom" passages as late. This is understandable in light of the wisdom tradition's later interest in and use of Jeremiah's teachings. This would be somewhat analogous to the similar interest of the later Deuteronomic authors. Not all of the evidence cited below will be universally accepted as reflecting the prophet's particular teachings. Nevertheless we must present the evidence which seems most probably associated with the prophet in an effort to determine how and why the wisdom tradition is utilized. Whatever conclusions are reached, we must integrate them into the picture stemming from an evaluation of the Deuteronomic movement (see Ch. V) so important to any analysis of the Book of Jeremiah as a whole.

Many literary forms and styles found in Jeremiah have been compared to analogous forms and styles in the wisdom literature. One of the most thorough studies has focused on Jeremiah's use of rhetorical questions, a stylistic device.

> Does the snow of Lebanon leave
>   the crags of Sirion?
> Do the mountain waters run dry,
>   the cold flowing streams? (18:14)

> Is Israel a slave? Is he a homeborn servant?
>   Why then has he become a prey? (2:14)

> "When men fall, do they not rise again?
>   If one turns away, does he not return?
> Why then has this people turned away
>   in perpetual backsliding?" (8:4-5)

As in other examples of prophetic rhetorical questions, Jeremiah uses these questions, usually based on obvious experiential observations, to stress the unnaturalness of Israel's response to or perception of Yahweh (cf. also 2:31, 3:5, 14:19, etc.). Though parallels of a thematic and formal nature are noted, the prophet's use of these questions presupposes a different kind of relationship between God and people than that of the wisdom tradition. Nevertheless, while the present function of these passages cannot be termed pedagogical, the power of these sayings rests not on an appeal to prophetic *dabar,* but rather is based on the obvious experiential legitimation/authority in the sayings themselves.

Jeremiah also makes use of many proverbial forms, though always adapting them to his message.[35]

> "You shall speak to them this word: 'Thus says the Lord, the God of Israel, "Every jar shall be filled with wine." ' And they will say to you, 'Do we not indeed know that every jar will be filled with wine?' Then you shall say to them, 'Thus says the Lord: Behold I will fill

with drunkenness all the inhabitants of the land: the kings who sit on David's throne, the priests, the prophets, and all the inhabitants of Jerusalem. And I will dash them one against another, fathers and sons together says the LORD. I will not pity or spare or have compassion, that I should not destroy them.' " (13:12-14)

In this particular example the original intention of the proverb has been changed. It has been interpreted to mean something almost entirely the opposite, thus being integrated into the prophet's judgment of all of Jerusalem. Nevertheless, this passage presupposes a common knowledge of the usual intention of such a form (and thereby also those who are responsible for such a form and message). It would be difficult to identify with any precision the original setting and intention of this proverb or others (cf., e.g., 5:26-28, 8:6, 15:2-3, 23:28, etc.). Nevertheless it does appear to have provided legitimation of present cultural conditions, including probably the monarchical structures of the society. It is precisely this function and character of the tradition which Jeremiah attacks.

A number of other literary forms and styles associated with wisdom have been found in Jeremiah including: question and answer schema (1:11-12, 13, 24:3); numerical formulae (15:3); metaphorical speech (9:2, 51:20-23); and a wisdom poem (17:5-11). In addition to these, many themes or motifs commonly considered to be characteristic of wisdom are found. Among these are: a preoccupation with understanding, emphasizing man's lack of it (4:22, 8:7, 9:23-24, etc.); Yahweh as creator (10:12ff. [51:15ff.], 31:35ff.); concerns with retribution (12:1ff., 17:11); social justice (5:20-29); and drinking (35:6). Most of these are not particularly enlightening or convincing by themselves, but when seen together they begin to raise serious possibilities that Jeremiah was, like Isaiah, concerned to make his message heard by those considered "wise." Further, they indicate that the prophet used the forms and themes often associated with the wisdom tradition to make his point.

This becomes clearer when the evidence already cited is integrated with the occurrence of wisdom vocabulary and references to those who are "wise" or who possess offices or functions often identified with them. Both Brueggemann and Holladay, among others, have indicated a basic concern with "wisdom" and "understanding" by the prophet in chapters 4–9 and following.[36]

> "In that day, says the LORD, courage shall fail both kings and princes; the priests shall be appalled and the prophets astounded." (4:9)

> "For my people are foolish,
>   they know me not;
> they are stupid children,
>   they have no understanding.
> They are skilled in doing evil,
>   but how to do good they know not." (4:22)

> O LORD, do not thy eyes look for truth?
> Thou hast smitten them,
>   but they felt no anguish;
> thou hast consumed them,
>   but they refused to take correction. (5:3)

> "Hear this, O foolish and senseless people,
>   who have eyes, but see not,
>   who have ears, but hear not." (5:21)

And you shall say to them, "This is the nation that did not obey the voice of the LORD their God, and did not accept discipline; truth has perished; it is cut off from their lips." (7:28)

> "How can you say, 'We are wise,
>   and the law of the LORD is with us'?
> But behold, the false pen of the scribes
>   has made it into a lie.
> The wise men shall be put to shame,
>   they shall be dismayed and taken;
> lo, they have rejected the word of the LORD,
>   and what wisdom is in them?" (8:8-9)

Who is the man so wise that he can understand this? To whom has the mouth of the LORD spoken, that he may declare it? Why is the land ruined and laid waste like a wilderness, so that no one passes through? (9:12)

Thus says the LORD: "Let not the wise man glory in his wisdom, let not the mighty man glory in his might, let not the rich man glory in his riches; but let him who glories glory in this, that he understands and knows me, that I am the LORD who practice steadfast love, justice, and righteousness in the earth; for in these things I delight, says the LORD." (9:23-24)

Yet they did not listen or incline their ear, but stiffened their neck, that they might not hear and receive instruction. (17:23)

Then they said, "Come, let us make plots against Jeremiah, for the law shall not perish from the priest, nor counsel from the wise, nor the word from the prophet. Come, let us smite him with the tongue, and let us not heed any of his words." (18:18)

These judgments also apply to the "wise" in foreign nations.

Who would not fear thee, O King of the nations?
  For this is thy due;
for among all the wise ones of the nations
  and in all their kingdoms
  there is none like thee. (10:7)

Thus says the LORD of hosts:
"Is wisdom no more in Teman?
  Has counsel perished from the prudent?
  Has their wisdom vanished?" (49:7)

"A sword upon the Chaldeans, says the LORD,
  and upon the inhabitants of Babylon,
  and upon her princes and her wise men!
A sword upon the diviners,
  that they may become fools!" (50:35-36)

It would be foolhardy at this stage in our discussion to attempt a synthesis of the teachings in these passages and others which would identify the "wise" or provide a clarification of Jeremiah's complex use of the wisdom tradition. We would, however, agree with Brueggemann that Jeremiah was addressing what might be considered an "epistemological" crisis. Moreover, the advocates of the position which Jeremiah attacks are often to be identified with monarchical functionaries either by the tasks they perform *(sopherim)* or the view of the actions and demands of Yahweh which they espouse. It seems clear also that Jeremiah utilizes an idiom often found in wisdom literature (cf. especially *musar*, "correction/discipline") to demonstrate both the errors of the people and the way in which Yahweh will make known these errors in judgment. It seems that a good case might be made for the existence of government officials as an essential element in the sociological matrix of the wisdom tradition. However, Whybray has pointed to an important element in Jeremiah's message by noting the generalization of those who are wise to include all who do not perceive what Yahweh is not doing, and not simply those who might be in some technical way classified as the wise.[37] While Jeremiah's use of torah is probably dependent upon the Deuteronomic reform, it is also generalized and no longer allowed to be merely the property of the cult.[38] The role of the Deuteronomic reformers themselves and their interaction with the wisdom tradition as well as the influence of Isaiah, may be in part responsible for this.

In conclusion, Jeremiah surely reflects the use and influence of the wisdom tradition. As with Isaiah, the tradition is in some cases attacked, but more often it forms and teachings are utilized by the prophet to demonstrate his own conception of what is "wise," of what Yahweh is doing in late pre-exilic Judah. Jeremiah's concern is therefore not so much to ascribe wisdom to Yahweh as Isaiah had done; this is assumed. Rather, Jeremiah turns wisdom's message back upon itself. At the same time he sets all of this within a prophetic picture of Yahweh judging the people for their deeds and misconceptions of them. This is brought about partially by adherence to the tenets of legitimizers (cf. 8:8-12) who refuse to believe that what Yahweh has established he can, and will, also destroy. Once more, what has been found is not an incompatibility of theological perspectives between prophet and wisdom tradition. Rather, it is a judgment that, in its valid concern for what is wise and good, the wisdom tradition (as well as prophets and priests) has become too closely associated with contemporary structures and the ideologies associated with them. Jeremiah in one sense is calling those who are "wise" back to a perspective which recognizes the limitation of any human capacity or institution, creating the possibility for a more fully developed (though, as we have seen, already present) theological interpretation and grounding of the wisdom tradition.

Habakkuk

One commentator has found parallels between Habakkuk and the wisdom literature which may point to another connection between prophets and wisdom.[39] The theme of the prophet (theodicy), the dialogical style, vocabulary, the absence of oracular forms and the doctrine of election, and the structure of the book which begins with complaint and ends with theophany (cf. Job) are among the reasons given for this potential connection. Many of the parallels noted are with the so-called "skeptical" wisdom literature (Job, Ecclesiastes, Proverbs 30, etc.), which is usually seen as a later development in wisdom itself. When these observations about Habakkuk are connected to certain passages from Jeremiah (cf., e.g., 12:1-3), however, a hypothesis may be made which takes seriously the influence in the wisdom tradition of prophetic observations which refuse to affirm a simplistic retributional schema for the actions of Yahweh. Surely, on the one hand, Israel and Judah are judged and condemned as a result of their sin. On the other hand, rigid teachings which attempt to equate God's favor and blessing with obedience to law and to the maintenance of the God-given institutions of monarchy and cult will not explain the subsequent judgment of God, nor reflect what is "wise." It is difficult to posit concrete wisdom influence in Habakkuk, but certainly Gowan is correct in asserting that we have failed to see the complex nature of Israelite society and the interrelatedness of all its traditions by overcompartmentalizing them and neglecting the points they share in common.[40]

The Wisdom Tradition and the Pre-exilic Prophets

Before addressing the question of the nature and shape of the wisdom tradition in this period, a few observations concerning wisdom influence and the prophets are in order. It has often been maintained that clear boundaries between wisdom and prophecy must be drawn in order to determine influence. This is problematic for at least two reasons. First, it presupposes that one can and should isolate particular traditions in ancient Israelite religion. Second, it seems to put forth the notion that influence consists of the use of forms, themes, etc., which reflect the intentions and concerns of their original setting. Neither of these assumptions is affirmed by the evidence. Rather than pointing to the hopelessness of the task, however, this observation seems simply to argue against the notion of "influence" itself. The interrelationship of prophecy and wisdom reflects situations and a culture in which prophets borrowed freely from literary forms and theological concerns available to them, with which they shared much, but which they also felt free to attack, to change, and to correct when necessary. To be sure, such a picture does not lend itself easily to "influence," if this means direct literary and theological dependence which might result in almost identical positions. If influence is taken to mean the serious evaluation and use of particular perspectives stemming from current sociologically and historically defined traditions, however, then certainly the prophets were influenced by wisdom.

The appearance of literary forms, teachings, and vocabulary in vast quantities throughout the prophetic literature also makes it difficult to accept the thesis that the real issue between the prophets and the wise was one of authority. While there is certainly a difference between the prophet's "word" and the sage's "counsel," the attacks of Isaiah and Jeremiah on the "wise" do not revolve around these poles. As noted above, the basic disagreement seems to center on the ultimate basis of one's loyalty, whether state or nation or Yahweh. The widespread use of wisdom teaching may point to the possibility of a common ethic, or to the assumption of the role of counselor by the prophet. Thus, a dialogue between prophets and the wise witnesses to that which utilizes the theological perspectives of both while at the same time it radically questions the loyalties and subsequent positions of the wise. While we have agreed with Brueggemann that in some sense there is an epistemological crisis involved between prophets and the wise, it is perhaps too easy to believe this crisis deals with the method by which knowledge is acquired (revelation/reason, *dabar/ᶜeṣah*). Rather the crisis has to do with the *results* of prophetic *dabar* and wisdom *ᶜeṣah*, the final evaluation of state, king, and people, achieved by whatever means. Indeed, the prophets, utilizing the same experiential authority of proverbial sayings, as just one example, come to radically different conclusions. This reflects more the ground of their ultimate loyalty than the epistemological basis of their authoritative knowledge.

When the shape of the wisdom tradition in the pre-exilic prophetic period is examined, it is hardly surprising that a uniform, "orthodox" picture does not emerge. Sociologically there does seem to be a basic division between the wisdom inside and outside Jerusalem. Amos and Micah especially reflect concerns stemming from an ethos quite different from that of the monarchy. This is seen not only in thematic concerns but also in the fact that these two prophets are much less dependent on proverbial forms than even Hosea. To be sure, much of this popular/clan wisdom finds its way into wisdom literature. Nevertheless, the absence of references to the wise, and the adaptation of forms, motifs, et al., into a message directed against the monarchy, rather than into a debate with the wise, strengthens the differentiation made. Our lack of knowledge about the village life of Israelites in this period makes further description of this tradition difficult, but the role of the elders and the conflict over the values and practices of the city suggested by Wolff are appealing and not incompatible with the messages of these country prophets.

These conclusions are further developed by the picture of the wisdom tradition which is gained from Isaiah and Jeremiah. Initially, at least, we must closely associate wisdom with the monarchy and its institutions. References to scribes and the wise are often connected to pro-monarchical viewpoints. While we are unable to pinpoint any passage which definitively proves the existence of a "school" or some other means of training in and transmitting of wisdom, nevertheless the existence of such an institution or group remains a likely hypothesis. What is clear is the prophetic generalization of wisdom to all of the people. Thus wisdom is used and evaluated not simply from the narrow perspective of a "class." The maintenance of loyalty to the status quo, the confidence in monarchical structures, and a "Yahweh is with us" theological stance so often associated with the "wise" is seen to be a false perspective for all, regardless of the roots of this now popular notion.

Theologically, the wisdom tradition seems not to have changed much. The presence of wisdom forms and messages in the prophets makes it difficult to assume the wisdom tradition was non-Yahwistic or that its basis of authority was secular empiricism. The challenge of the prophets to the wisdom tradition is *not* to accept the authority of revelation. Rather, it is to forsake reliance upon the institutional structures which the wise, falsely, believes legitimates its perspectives, and to ascribe true wisdom to Yahweh alone. It is easy to see the difficulty the wise may have had in accepting such a message if not only their ideologies, but their food, is tied to the monarchy!

Wisdom was not static in this period. It was not a constant on which the prophets drew. Yahwistic and authoritative from the beginning, found in the court with counselors and other officials, disseminated to others in society, perhaps through scribes, also found in another form in the villages, it grew and changed, especially in the court (school?) circles responsible for Proverbs. Many studies have spoken of and demonstrated the prophets' reinterpretation of wisdom teaching in their conflict with the wise, especially the counselors of the king. In this process, however, many have characterized the wisdom tradition as static to a great extent, impervious (no doubt because of its empirical, worldly wise ways) to the attacks of the prophets. Such a picture, in light of all the prophetic material, seems unlikely. The wisdom tradition did indeed change; often this would take place in response to the prophetic reinterpretation and use of its teaching. Thus the concepts of ʿeṣah, torah and the notion of a class ethic were all changed by the prophetic use of them. To this extent one must speak of prophetic influence on the wise men, though hardly with the same patterns of development and theological perspective as in the past. This is hardly a surprising conclusion. Rather it is perfectly understandable if our notions of prophets and wise men and the messages of each are less rigid and, therefore, less unrealistic. To a certain extent, the prophets themselves have proposed a new dimension and a new emphasis for the wisdom tradition. In addition, the fall of Jerusalem and the monarchy, the emerging importance of the scribes as official transmitters of the "law," and the related influence of the Deuteronomic movement must all be considered important factors in the future development of the wisdom tradition.

CHAPTER V
WISDOM AND THE DEUTERONOMIC MOVEMENT

Similarities between the Deuteronomic literature (Deuteronomy and texts placed under the perspective of the Deuteronomistic "school") and wisdom literature have long been noted. But, for all the reasons cited in our discussion of pre-exilic prophetic literature above, until very recently it has been assumed that Deuteronomic literature had influenced the *later* wisdom literature. However, a sizable number of important studies now maintain precisely the opposite position: that Deuteronomy contains wisdom perspectives which have been changed in light of new circumstances.[1] Part of the reason for the change in perspective, the change in the direction of influence, has to do with the increasing number of scholars who, in the light of ancient Near Eastern parallels and the wisdom influence manifested by other pre-Deuteronomic, non-wisdom traditions, refuse to confine all wisdom literature to the exilic period. Equally important, however, has been the continued focus on the Deuteronomic period and movement as seminal in the history of Israelite religion. To a certain extent one might characterize recent studies in source criticism,[2] covenant,[3] and Deuteronomic literature[4] as attempts to transpose von Rad's thesis of change and development, "enlightenment," from the Solomonic period to the seventh century. There are many different motivations, as well as some textual ambiguity, associated with such a move. From our perspective, it is clear that such studies are quite compatible with a certain view of the wisdom tradition.[5] It cannot be denied that scribes and the "wise" as official functionaries appear more frequently from the reign of Hezekiah on (cf. Prov. 25:1). Furthermore, the anonymity of the transmitters of the peculiar Deuteronomic perspective creates the possibility and opportunity for the scribes, immersed in the wisdom perspective, to be the central figures in this "reform." The recent focus on treaty terminology and structure for covenant has allowed Weinfeld, for example, to free Deuteronomy from an exclusively cultic and/or prophetic provenance and to posit a setting quite compatible with the wisdom tradition as seen, to this point, in our study: namely, scribal circles close to the monarchical institution.

Before the evidence for wisdom in the Deuteronomic corpus is presented, a few observations are in order. First, no one maintains that Deuteronomic literature is wisdom literature. Rather, its authors are thought to be closely associated with the circles which are responsible for the particular theological perspectives found in wisdom literature. Therefore we are, as in the case of the prophets, dealing with wisdom influence, with material which may be reflective of the social setting and provenance not simply of scribes but also of the wisdom tradition upon which they were dependent. Second, the implications of some positions held regarding wisdom and Deuteronomy, mostly notably that of Weinfeld, are very important for the resultant picture of the development of Israelite religion. However, we must be careful to be sensitive to the possibility that the particular picture of Israelite religion gained by finding wisdom antecedent to Deuteronomy may not be the result of our conclusions, but rather the presupposition!

Third, and finally, if our picture of the wisdom tradition and its interrelationship with other non-wisdom traditions in ancient Israel to this point has any merit, then in all probability to posit wisdom influencing Deuteronomy or Deuteronomy influencing wisdom is at best oversimplified. The fact that the Deuteronomic movement has been associated with the prophetic movement and the monarchy makes it almost impossible to assume that the wisdom tradition would not be found, in view of its association with prophets and kings in the past. But in all probability the issue is not one of influence as much as of growth, development, and interaction. Still, what arises at this time more than earlier periods is the strong association of particular wisdom perspectives with a sociologically definable group called the wise, or scribes. To this point in the history of Israelite religion such discussions have been much less comprehensive than they are when the Deuteronomic period is evaluated.[6]

Those scholars who associate Deuteronomy with wisdom literature, usually with a scribal provenance, are dependent on the assumptions that: (1) a sociologically definable group of *sopherim* did indeed exist at this time; and (2) that the scribes can be in some way connected both with wisdom and with the Deuteronomic movement. While many Old Testament passages and ancient Near Eastern parallels are cited, perhaps no book is more important than Jeremiah for this purpose. The roles of Shaphan, presumed to be the head of a scribal circle, Baruch (cf. Jer. 36), and the long recognized Deuteronomic redaction of the book are important clues in the identification of the provenance of the Deuteronomic movement.[7]

The explanation of the functions and teachings of the scribes is still dependent to a large degree upon our knowledge of parallel phenomena from Egypt, for little explicit reference is found in the Old Testament. In Jeremiah and Deuteronomy, however, the scribes are associated with the torah (Deut. 33:10, Jer. 8:8). The debated passage, Jeremiah 8:8-9, is of special importance, for here the scribes are not only seen to be identified with the torah but with the wise as well.

> How can you say, "We are wise,
>   and the law of the LORD is with us"?
> But, behold, the false pen of the scribes
>   has made it into a lie.

> The wise men shall be put to shame,
>   they shall be dismayed and taken;
> lo, they have rejected the word of the LORD,
>   and what wisdom is in them?

Whether we identify torah with Deuteronomy in this passage as Weinfeld has done,[8] the scribes, the wise, and the responsibility for interpretation of torah seem to be tied together.[9] The precise role of the scribes in the formulation of Deuteronomic literature, their connection with the elusive *ḥakamim,* and their role in the transmission of torah, however defined, must be evaluated after the evidence in the Deuteronomic literature has been examined.

Interestingly enough, the influence of the wisdom tradition is not found primarily in literary forms which the Deuteronomic movement utilizes, but rather in rhetoric, style, motifs, vocabulary, organizational format, and intention. An exception to this is the indirect reference in 1 Kings 5:12-13 to various wise sayings of Solomon and potential parallels in Prov. 30:15-33.

One of the most striking characteristics of Deuteronomy and Deuteronomic literature is its exhortatory style. While this style has often been associated with the preaching of the prophets or the cult, many recent studies have questioned this potential setting or provenance and proposed a scribal, literary origin instead.[10] Such a setting presupposes a connection between scribes and torah, and maintains this exhortatory style as best interpreted, at least in part, as wisdom instruction.

> "When your son asks you in time to come, 'What is the meaning of the testimonies and the statutes and the ordinances which the LORD our God has commanded you?' then you shall say to your son, 'We were Pharaoh's slaves in Egypt; and the LORD brought us out of Egypt with a mighty hand; and the LORD showed signs and wonders, great and grievous, against Egypt and against Pharaoh and all his household, before our eyes; and he brought us out from there, that he might bring us in and give us the land which he swore to give to our fathers. And the LORD commanded us to do all these statutes, to fear the LORD our God, for our good always, that he might preserve

us alive, as at this day. And it will be righteousness for us, if we are careful to do all this commandment before the LORD our God, as he has commanded us.'" (Deut. 6:20-25)

While the content of this particular instruction cannot be equated easily with that of wisdom literature, the father-son relationship[11] and the didactic intention (cf. also 1 Kings 8) point to a wisdom tradition idiom and intention. This has been separated from its original setting (at least the father-son schema) and used to speak of and frame national, political, cultic concerns. If the scribes are closely associated with the institutions of the state, as indeed the major wisdom traditions traced to this point have been, then there is little difficulty in attributing such concerns to wisdom.

It remains to be seen, however, why a didactic intention is particularly representative of the wisdom tradition alone. The utilization of a father-son (teacher-pupil) relationship to authorize and explain the passing down of sacred tradition and knowledge (cf. Deut. 4) from generation to generation is a stronger argument. Many scholars have noted the use of this relationship in wisdom literature throughout the ancient Near East. Closely connected to this phenomenon of wisdom instruction in exhortatory style is the observation that such teaching is attributed to national heroes (Moses, David, Solomon, Hezekiah, Jeremiah) who perform a similar legitimizing function to those royal figures in ancient Near Eastern wisdom.[12]

In addition to attributing a basic Deuteronomic literary characteristic to a wisdom, scribal setting, much other stylistic evidence is cited. Reference to the rhetorical technique of the scribes, the use of motive clauses, organizational schemas similar to those of proverbial wisdom, and autobiographical reminiscence (Deut. 4:21-22) is also made in an effort to identify scribes, wisdom, and Deuteronomy with each other (partially).[13]

In addition to the use of proverbial and stylistic similarities, a number of themes and concerns in Deuteronomy are mentioned as characteristic of wisdom's teaching. Perhaps the two most often cited examples of this are the laws concerning landmarks and weights and measures.

"You shall not remove your neighbor's landmark, which the men of old have set." (Deut. 19:14)	Remove not the ancient landmark which your fathers have set. (Prov. 22:28) Do not remove an ancient landmark or enter the fields of the fatherless. (Prov. 23:10)
"You shall not have in your bag two kinds of weights, a large and a small. You shall not have in your house two kinds of measures, a large and a small. A full and just weight you shall have. . . . For all who do such things, all who act dishonestly, are an abomination to the LORD your God." (Deut. 25:13-16)	A false balance is an abomination to the LORD, but a just weight is his delight. (Prov. 11:1) Diverse weights are an abomination to the LORD, and false scales are not good. (Prov. 20:23)

It is the similar phraseology which makes these parallels significant and suggests the strong possibility of dependence. Both Weinfeld and Carmichael, utilizing different arguments, maintain that the passages in Deuteronomy are dependent upon a wisdom tradition's earlier proverbial formulation[14] (cf. the study of L'Hour and the concept of to⁽ebah).

Many other content-oriented thematic and rhetorical parallels are noted.[15]

"You shall not add to the word which I command you, nor take from it." (Deut. 4:2)	Every word of God proves true. . . . Do not add to his words, lest he rebuke you, and you be found a liar. (Prov. 30:5-6)
"Everything that I command you you shall be careful to do; you shall not add to it or take from it." (Deut. 13:1 [12:32 Eng.]; cf. Jer. 26:2)	Whatever God does endures for ever; nothing can be added to it, nor anything taken from it. (Eccles. 3:14; cf. Ben Sira 18:6; 42:21)

"When you make a vow to the LORD your God, you shall not be slack to pay it; for the LORD your God will surely require it of you, and it would be sin in you. But if you refrain from vowing, it shall be no sin in you. You shall be careful to perform what has passed your lips . . . what you have promised with your mouth." (Deut. 23:21-23)

Be not rash with your mouth, nor let your heart be hasty to utter a word before God. . . When you vow a vow to God, do not delay in paying it; for he has no pleasure in fools. Pay what you vow. It is better that you should not vow than that you should vow and not pay. Let not your mouth lead you into sin. (Eccles. 5:2-6 [Eng. 5:1-4])

It is a snare for a man to say rashly, "It is holy," and to reflect only after making his vows. (Prov. 20:25; cf. Ben Sira 18:22)

Numerous other examples have been cited which attempt to demonstrate a concern in Deuteronomic literature with themes and motifs found in wisdom literature. The presence of much wisdom vocabulary is also noted.[16]

Although some of the arguments and observations made above warrant a serious consideration of a scribal provenance for Deuteronomic literature associated with the wisdom tradition, these arguments are generally not conclusive. There are, however, three larger, more comprehensive characteristics of the Deuteronomic corpus which indicate a definite connection with wisdom and point to more identifiable and peculiar aspects of the wisdom tradition itself. These are: humanism, torah, and retribution. The humanistic nature of the Deuteronomic laws has long been observed. A comparison with antecedent laws dealing with identical concerns in the Covenant Code, for example, reflects the change from a "narrow law corpus to humanistic law."[17] New concerns with morality and social intercourse are found throughout. While the influence of the prophetic movement can and has been seen as the source of this humanism, Weinfeld and others who argue for a wisdom (scribal) tradition more closely associated with the monarchical structures are far more convincing. It would be inappropriate and simplistic to attribute "humanism" to the wisdom tradition alone, although this aspect of the tradition has often been highlighted by scholars in the past. The peculiar nature of Deuteronomic literature with its focus on monarchy, cult, and the state, however, makes an association with wisdom far more likely and probable than other interpretations available.

The use and meaning of torah in Deuteronomic literature also suggests a wisdom/scribal provenance. Torah in Deuteronomy does not refer primarily or even usually to the cultic regulations given by Yahweh to his people. This particular meaning of torah is found in the Priestly Code. Rather, torah "is the word employed by the Deuteronomic editors to convey their concept of the code as a complete expression of the will of God."[18] Weinfeld maintains that this particular meaning does not come directly from the cult but rather from the treaty typology used in Deuteronomy. This typology stresses the loyalty of a covenant partner to the great sovereign rather than the observance of precepts within every area of life.[19] These observations about torah are usually connected to the didactic character of the law and the intention that an appropriate understanding of torah is necessary both to explain the vicissitudes of the monarchy and to ensure its existence.

Closely connected to torah in Deuteronomic literature is the doctrine of reward or retribution so commonly associated with this literature. To be sure, such a perspective or connection is found in other traditions. Nevertheless, some of the observations made above point to a specific connection between Deuteronomic and wisdom traditions here. Weinfeld and others observe parallels between wisdom literature and Deuteronomy regarding life and good, possession of the land, and theodicy.[20] Even more convincing is the association of the "good" which Yahweh bestows upon a nation obedient to his torah with the concerns and vested interests of those closely associated with the state. Surely different settings and purposes must be attributed to the transmitters of Proverbs and Deuteronomy, but the common retributional framework witnesses to traditions which are legitimated by and legitimize the same basic authoritative institution: a monarchy.

The conclusions concerning the relationship of the Deutero- nomic corpus of the wisdom tradition have many implications for the shape and nature of the latter. If a scribal circle is responsible for Deuteronomy and its perspective is to be associated with that of the wisdom tradition, then for the first time we are able to identify clearly one part of its social setting. It must first be noted that all conclusions concerning the authorship of Deuteronomic material remain suppositional. There is still no Old Testament witness which explicitly identifies the authors. Moreover, when the wise (*ḥakamim*) or the scribes (*sopherim*) are discussed, we cannot be sure exactly what the functions and teachings of these groups were. Surely several groups were called "wise" and not all scribes are considered so. Having admitted the necessary tenuousness of our conclusions, it still seems a most probable and attractive hypothesis that scribes, connected to and in some sense carriers of the wisdom tradition, were involved in the composition of the Deuteronomic material. The role of Shaphan, the probable function and place of the scribe based on ancient Near Eastern (especially Egyptian) parallels, the concerns of Deuteronomy with judicial and monarchi- cal issues, the recasting of many institutional practices in humanistic form, and the presence of much material found also and, often, primarily in wisdom literature, all point to such a conclusion.

Whether or not the scribal circle responsible for Deuteronomic literature was the product of royal "schools" or just a group of literate officials remains an open question. Surely we must be cautious in reconstructing institutions and organizations without explicit mention of them. But the Deuteronomic corpus itself is a witness to some group and the nature of the evidence points to scribes as more probable than Levites or prophets.

To conclude that the scribes were responsible for Deuteronomy sometimes carries with it a thesis that, because of the literary quality of the composition, this circle was detached from the political life of the nation. We would suggest precisely the opposite. The subject matter and intention of the Deuteronomic corpus indicates a group with a vested interest in the present and future of Jerusalem and Israel as a whole. The authors of these texts were not "wise men" whose primary task was to write proverbial wisdom, though they were probably closely associated with the teachings of the wisdom tradition found in proverbial form. They not only reflected the influence of wisdom teaching but also had concerns for the cult. The influence of the prophets is also probable.

To the extent, therefore, that the social setting can be identified, it must be located in the midst of all the major voices of the period and is characterized by an overarching concern to assimilate and relate such voices in a new message to the people. Ultimately the response of these authors is characterized by a close connection with the institutional entities of the monarchy and permeated by the language and concerns of the wisdom tradition. This does not allow us to classify Deuteronomy as wisdom, but it does witness to a tradition close to the monarchy, concerned with many different facets of public life, and utilized by scribal functionaries.

Although we must wait until the end of this study to reach fuller conclusions, it appears that perhaps Whybray is at least partially correct when he fails to find a "class" of the wise in Israel. However, the commonality of perspective and teaching between wisdom literature and Deuteronomy indicates groups which share common perspectives and compatible functions. It is difficult to attribute such commonality to merely intellectual literary activity. Rather, the distinct literary forms, theological perspectives, and attachment to the monarchy witness to a tradition which demands and warrants a more definite sociological setting and a more clearly delineated and differentiated worldview than Whybray allows for.

It is recognized by all commentators on Deuteronomy that its authors utilize many sources and perspectives not their own. What, however, do the scribes bring to their task which can aid us in our attempt to define more fully the nature of the wisdom tradition? If Weinfeld is correct, one contribution of the scribes is the treaty typology into which the book is fitted. This perspective, with its focus on obedience to the sovereign, while compatible with wisdom teaching, is more valuable in affirming the social setting of the scribes, namely the monarchy where such forms and ideology would be in common use. The use of torah, with its dependence on such treaty typology, and the concern with instruction rather than enumeration of precepts, is also to be associated with the wisdom tradition and the scribes. It is not inconceivable that this use of torah was already in some sense influenced by Isaiah and other prophets who maintained that God and not man is the giver of right instruction. In any case, the Deuteronomic material witnesses to the responsibility the scribes felt for the torah, an important factor in the development both of the office of scribes and the equation of wisdom and torah in later periods.

Whether it is appropriate to utilize the term "secular," the authors of Deuteronomic literature reflect an interest and concern for all aspects of life and a tendency to free law from narrow cultic perspectives, replacing them with national, humanistic ones. When this is compared with wisdom literature, one sees both a compatibility in terms of attitudes toward the cult and humanistic perspectives as well as, potentially, the germ of future development in the nationalization of wisdom found in later apocryphal wisdom literature.

Deuteronomy is often seen to be indicative of a new movement, a new development, in the history of Israelite religion. Coupled with this is the thesis that, due to the peculiar perspectives of this movement, the wisdom tradition itself was changed. In order to evaluate this claim a statement of Weinfeld may be used as an illustration.

Thus the Hezekiah period, which marked the beginning of Deuteronomic literary activity, is not to be regarded as the period in which the traditions concerning Solomonic wisdom first crystallized, as Scott argues, but as one which marks a historical turning point in the development of the Israelite conception of wisdom. During this period, which is marked by a resurgence of intellectual literary activity, the concept "wisdom" had taken on a new meaning which accorded with the new temper of the times. The Deuteronomist no longer conceived of "wisdom" as meaning cunning, pragmatic talent, or the possession of extraordinary knowledge, but held it to be synonymous with the knowledge and understanding of proper behaviour and with morality.[21]

This view of the development of wisdom is at least partially compatible with traditional explanations of the diversity of perspectives found within wisdom literature itself. Moreover, it does not presuppose a static unchanging tradition but rather one which adapts and develops theologically. We would agree that there appears to be an increased concern with morality in Deuteronomy, but this seems to be a matter of degree, not of kind. If wisdom was ever seen to be merely cunning or pragmatic talent, it was, from the very beginning of the monarchy, quickly placed within theological traditions which provided many other dimensions.

What appears to be the most significant factor in the development of the wisdom tradition in the Deuteronomic period is the amalgamation of various wisdom and non-wisdom perspectives into a truly nationalistic group of writings. Wisdom has most often been associated with the monarchy, and the prophets had criticized it for this. Deuteronomic literature reflects a use of wisdom which on the one hand still clings to the institutions of the state as the hope for the future while at the same time utilizing its torah, its instruction, to relativize the absolute claims of these institutions and direct their concerns to the nation, the people. It is difficult to see such a development as "new," for it rests on the loyalties of the past (Ch. III) as well as the prophetic critiques leveled against such loyalty, also in the past.

It remains to be seen what will happen when the institutions of the state are dissolved in the exile, but the developments reflected in the Deuteronomic literature give a clue to the extent that the monarchy is no longer the sole focus, but only one means by which the torah of Yahweh may be made known.

CHAPTER VI
WISDOM IN THE EXILE

Recent Old Testament scholarship, particularly biblical theology, has focused a great deal of its attention on the exile.[1] Rather than viewing the exilic period as a time of mourning, or destruction and disintegration of societal structures and ideologies, this period has been characterized as the time of birth for a new religion, Judaism. Of course, within this period Isaiah 40–55 and much of Ezekiel have always been seen as high points for the future development of the history of Israel. But now the exile is also the time of the Priestly Code and with it the final structure of the Pentateuch (Torah), the initial formulation of the Chronicler's history, the Deuteronomistic history, Lamentations, many psalms, etc. Thus the exile has become a period when a pluralistic response was made to the catastrophe of 587 B.C., and a model for many who perceive a similar situation in these "post-modern," "post-Constantinian," "post-neo-orthodox" times. In some ways, one can link together the present popularity of both wisdom and the exile, for the former provides a different way of doing theology and constructing the biblical message while the latter provides a sociological model in which to do theology and a justification for examining this particular perspective. While there is some warrant for these developments in contemporary scholarship, our study to this point would argue against any dichotomy made between the theological perspectives of wisdom and more "normative" traditions, stressing instead the common Yahwistic matrix of theology and society out of which they come. At the same time a study of wisdom and non-wisdom traditions in the pre-exilic period demonstrates many characteristics, concerns, and antecedants of the pluralism found in the exile, making it unnecessary to utilize this period as the only or best model for doing theology in our time.

Nevertheless, it is clear that the exile is important in our study of the wisdom tradition. With the institutions of state and monarchy destroyed, this period witnessed the beginning of new social and ideological structures which will ultimately provide wisdom with a base for the future. Two points are important here. First, as in earlier periods, there is little textual evidence which aids us in determining precisely and clearly the social setting of wisdom in this time or even the sociological base for the future. Second, our study of wisdom in the pre-exilic prophets and in the Deuteronomic movement has already witnessed to significant changes and developments within the wisdom tradition beginning in the eighth and seventh centuries. Therefore, while the fall of Judah and the exilic experiences in Babylon and Jerusalem are very important factors in the development of Israelite religion in general and wisdom in particular, we would be oversimplifying the situation to attribute changes in perspective only to the exile. Much of the development of wisdom can only be seen by viewing wisdom's interrelationship and integration with other non-wisdom traditions long before the exile. The common belief in early twentieth century scholarship that, for example, "later" wisdom is influenced by prophetic thought and literary forms must be evaluated in light of a long-standing relationship between prophets and wisdom in the pre-exilic period.

Despite the fact that the exile is seen by many to have provided an impetus for the basic theological structure of many Old Testament sources,[2] only three of these have been clearly associated with and seen to be dependent upon the wisdom tradition: Ezekiel, the Priestly Code, and Isaiah 40–55. Of these three sources, Isaiah 40–55 is perhaps most significant in terms of theological parallels with wisdom. Nevertheless, Ezekiel and the Priestly Code can be important in determining the guidelines for sociological developments within Israelite society which provide both ideological and institutional bases for the future development of the wise man/scribe.

Ezekiel

Study of the Book of Ezekiel occasions much debate concerning the setting of the prophet (Jerusalem and/or Babylon), the number and date of sources *not* to be attributed to the prophet himself, and other critical questions difficult to answer.[2] When the wisdom influence found in the book is evaluated, however, many of these debates are not raised. While Ezekiel does not manifest the amount of contact with the wisdom tradition found in Isaiah of Jerusalem and Jeremiah, those passages which do reflect the use of the wisdom tradition show a continuity of perspective, content, and form which is compatible with the results of our study to this point. The fact that the monarchy no longer exists, as well as the overt priestly concerns of the prophet, may explain at least part of the reason why so little wisdom is found. Nevertheless, what is found witnesses to a definite contact with and use of the tradition as delineated above.

Ezekiel makes reference to and use of several proverbial sayings.

> "Son of Man, what is this proverb that you have about the land of Israel saying, 'The days grow long, and every vision comes to nought?'" (12:22)

> "Son of Man, how does the wood of the vine surpass any wood, the vine branch which is among the trees of the forest?" (15:2ff.)

> "Behold, everyone who uses proverbs will use this proverb about you, 'Like mother, like daughter.'" (16:44)

> "What do you mean by repeating this proverb concerning the land of Israel, 'The fathers have eaten sour grapes, and the children's teeth are set on edge'?" (18:2)

It is important to notice the different uses made of these sayings. Ezekiel 15:2, while being part of a larger allegory, is by itself much like a riddle in character. As with the proverb in 16:44, also set in the context of an allegory, this saying is used to stress the message of Yahweh from a positive perspective. The proverbs in chapters 12 and 16, however, are ostensibly the cause and occasion for correcting a mistaken impression of the people concerning the actions of Yahweh toward his people. The proverb is wrong! Perhaps Ezekiel 18:3 is the best commentary and illustration of this use of proverbs by Ezekiel: "As I live, says the Lord GOD, this proverb shall no more be used by you in Israel." This use of proverbial sayings not only reflects a familiarity with such sayings in the exile, but more importantly demonstrates the ability of the prophet to incorporate a message into a prophetic speech as well as a conflict between the popular understandings presupposed by these particular sayings.

Ezekiel, as noted in Chapter II, makes use of allegories which may have been a "popular" wisdom form.

> "Son of man, propound a riddle, and speak an allegory to the house of Israel." (17:2)

> Then I said, "Ah Lord GOD! they are saying of me, 'Is he not a maker of allegories?'" (20:49)

Such a view once more connects the prophet with a knowledge and acquaintance with such forms and their peculiar perspectives, although he does not always affirm the message.

Many scholars have pointed to Ezek. 28:1-10 or portions thereof in discussing wisdom and Ezekiel.

> "Son of man, say to the prince of Tyre, Thus says the Lord GOD:
> "Because your heart is proud,
>   and you have said, 'I am a god,
> I sit in the seat of the gods,
>   in the heart of the seas,'
> yet you are but a man, and no god,
>   though you consider yourself as wise as a god—

> you are indeed wiser than Daniel;
>   no secret is hidden from you;
> by your wisdom and your understanding
>   you have gotten wealth for yourself,
> and have gathered gold and silver into
>   your treasuries;
> by your great wisdom in trade
>   you have increased your wealth,
>   and your heart has become proud in your wealth—
> therefore thus says the Lord GOD:
> "Because you consider yourself
>   as wise as a god,
> therefore, behold, I will bring strangers upon you,
>   the most terrible of the nations;
> and they shall draw their swords against the beauty of your wisdom
>   and defile your splendor." (28:2-7)

While this passage is clearly against the foreign wisdom of Tyre, it has much more in common with Isaiah and Jeremiah. Though it would be difficult to assume wisdom in Israel was like wisdom in Tyre on the basis of this passage alone, connections between wisdom and the monarchy in both nations may be noted. More than this, the critique of the prophet stands against a wisdom which perceives itself to be self-sufficient, seeing itself separate and valid apart from its source. These critiques are in a line with those of earlier prophets.

In view of the use and familiarity with proverbial teachings which seem to come from a popular versus a monarchical ethos, the following passage takes on special significance.

> "Disaster comes upon disaster, rumor follows rumor; they seek a vision from the prophet, but the law perishes from the priest, and counsel from the elders." (7:26)

Unlike Jeremiah and Isaiah, ʿeṣah is not ascribed to the wise, usually associated with monarchical circles, but to the elders (zᵉkenim), those often found responsible for justice at the city gate, in the smaller towns and villages of Israel. Two important points may be noted here. First, this passage provides at least part of the rationale for Ezekiel's use of and attack upon wisdom, for it is clear that no longer will these sources of direction or guidance be adequate in light of the occupation of the land. Secondly, such a passage underlines the absence of "official" wisdom and sets the stage for the popular understandings of the exile which Ezekiel at one and the same time attacks and incorporates into his own message. The wisdom tradition may have lost one of its primary sociological settings with the monarchy, but the experiential perception of what God is doing formulated through aphoristic forms and idioms continues, and is utilized by the prophet himself. The mention of "elders" in chapter seven does not point necessarily to "clan wisdom," but with other evidence from the book does indicate a loosening of the tradition from its institutional base. At the same time a continued use of wisdom forms and thought to aid in the understanding of the present calamity is witnessed to by the text.

The Priestly Creation Story: Genesis 1

In light of the commonly held view that "wisdom theology is creation theology," it is not surprising that the influence of wisdom is sometimes found in Genesis 1.[5] The passage usually associated with Genesis 1 is Proverbs 8:22-31.

> The Lord created me at the beginning of his work,
>   the first of his acts of old.
> Ages ago I was set up,
>   at the first, before the beginning of the earth.
> When there were no depths I was brought forth,
>   when there were no springs abounding with water.
> Before the mountains had been shaped,
>   before the hills, I was brought forth;
> before he had made the earth with its fields,
>   or the first of the dust of the world.
> When he established the heavens, I was there,
>   when he drew a circle on the face of the deep,
> when he made firm the skies above,
>   when he established the fountains of the deep,

> when he assigned to the sea its limit,
>> so that the waters might not transgress his command,
> when he marked out the foundations of the earth,
>> then I was beside him, like a master workman;
> and I was daily his delight,
>> rejoicing before him always,
> rejoicing in his inhabited world
>> and delighting in the sons of men.

While similarities in vocabulary exist, there are far more differences than points in common in these two passages. The thesis that one is dependent upon the other is difficult, if not impossible, to justify. Nevertheless, Landes has pointed to the "possibility" of indirect wisdom influence in the plant distinctions (Gen. 1:11-12) "which may go back to the kind of observations and classifications associated with the activity of the wise men," and also in the "list of natural phenomena and constituents of the cosmos."[5] A more general similarity has been found by Brueggemann, who focuses on Gen. 1:27-31 and stresses that the picture of man having dominion and responsibility over the created order (with the commensurate skill necessary to fulfill this responsibility) is compatible and even to be associated with that of the wisdom literature.[6]

We have already noted above that wisdom has had an interest in creation from at least the early monarchical period (Ch. III). Confirmation of this is suggested by recent studies of Prov. 8:22-31 which propose an early origin for this passage.[7] Nevertheless, the conceptions about the origin of these creation traditions ultimately point to quite different theological purposes and provenances. Still, if Crenshaw's belief that creation theology is utilized by the wisdom tradition to speak to particular problems, to defend the notion of God's presence and justice in a world seemingly without it, is correct, we must not separate the theological purposes of the Priestly Code and the wisdom tradition too dramatically.[8] Regardless of the date of Proverbs 8, and of the dependence or lack thereof of Genesis 1 upon wisdom, the focus on creation by the

Priestly Code signals a theological development essential for the
Israelite understanding of the exile and its aftermath. Moreover,
the presence and use of the wisdom tradition in Second Isaiah is
another indicator of the growth and development of this tradition
itself.

Isaiah 40–55

The setting for this unknown prophet is almost universally
recognized to be Babylon (cf., e.g., 44:28ff.). The prophet utilizes
many literary forms usually associated with cultic worship. This has
been seen to indicate both a source of his message and the setting for
his proclamation. Many comparisons between Second Isaiah and
the wisdom literature have been made. Among the more significant
examples cited are the use of proverbial forms (cf. 49:24; 55:8, 13
[Instead of the thorn shall come up the cypress; instead of the briar
shall come up the myrtle]); woe oracles utilizing natural, experiential
comparisons and connected to an oracle using God's creative power
as the answer to those upon whom woes were pronounced (45:9f.);
and the series of questions concerning the creator (40:12ff., cf. Job
38ff. [a stylistic observation]) enclosed in a prophetic disputation
speech containing wisdom vocabulary and concerns.[9]

More important that these observations, however, are the
thematic parallels noted. The conception of God as creator is
extremely important for this prophet.

> Thus says God, the LORD,
>> who created the heavens and then stretched them out,
>> who spread forth the earth and what comes from it,
> who gives breath to the people upon it
>> and spirit to those who walk in it (42:5)

> Thus says the LORD, your Redeemer,
>> who formed you from the womb:
> "I am the LORD, who made all things,
>> who stretched out the heavens alone,
>> who spread out the earth—Who was with me?" (44:24)

I form light and create darkness,
  I make weal and create woe,
I am the LORD, who do all these things. (45:7)

I made the earth,
  and created man upon it;
it was my hands that stretched out the heavens,
  and I commanded all their host. (45:12)

"My hand laid the foundation of the earth,
  and my right hand spread out the heavens;
When I call to them,
  they stand forth together." (48:13)

The extent to which God is seen as creator represents a new development in prophetic thought. In view of an inability to point to the monarchy, state, or cult, this prophet's focus on the whole of the created order is a natural one. At the same time it witnesses to a vision of Yahweh which far transcends the bounds of most of the prophet's contemporaries. Creation is not used by the prophet to inform his people of the rudiments of salvation history, but rather it reflects the power (cf., e.g., 40:15, 17, 26; 43:13) of God and the finiteness of man (cf. especially 45:9ff.) It ultimately provides the rationale or framework for a message which proclaims the seemingly impossible, that Yahweh will indeed comfort his people and deliver them from exile. It is important to note that while the notion of God as creator stresses the finiteness of man, it also releases him from a purely nationalistic focus and provides all the created order as the matrix within which theologizing may, indeed *must,* be done. There is also an emphasis upon the wisdom of God by this prophet, sometimes connected to creation or to the hiddenness of God.

(Yahweh) who frustrates the omens of liars,
  and makes fools of diviners;
who turns wise men back,
  and makes their knowledge foolish;
who confirms the word of his servant,
  and performs the counsel of his messengers;

who says of Jerusalem, "She shall be inhabited,"
   and of the cities of Judah, "They shall be built,
   and I will raise up their ruins." (44:25-26)

Thus says the LORD,
   the Holy One of Israel, and his Maker:
"Will you question me about my children,
   or command me concerning the work of my hands?" (45:11)

In these passages we find both a continuity with earlier prophetic teaching which attributes wisdom's source and authority to Yahweh alone *and* an integration of this message into a creator God framework which we have noted is characteristic of this prophet. Just as those who are "wise" did not know what Yahweh was doing in the pre-exilic period, so too the scope of Yahweh's actions transcends man's understanding in the exile. This is not a denial of wisdom's teachings or perspectives, but rather a positive use of themes and motifs common to prophets and wisdom (cf., e.g., Qoheleth, for a negative evaluation of these themes and concerns). Some commentators have pointed to Isa. 50:10 and 51:7 as examples of the use of the "fear of the LORD" and torah which are compatible with the wisdom tradition. The focus on obedience rather than particular cultic precepts is harmonious with similar teaching in Deuteronomy, for example, though the passages involved are not extensive or explicit enough to warrant further development of this connection.

There have been a number of important individual studies relating Isaiah 40–55 to the wisdom tradition. Pfeiffer and Terrien have both studied the numerous parallels between Job and this prophet.[10] Although their positions are similar, we will focus on Terrien's study which is far more detailed and persuasive. Terrien begins with the supposition that Job was written before Second Isaiah. In order to demonstrate the validity of this supposition, Terrien presents and examines numerous parallels between the two works. He notes similarities in vocabulary and idiom as Pfeiffer had done before him, but then makes a detailed comparison of three different motifs found in both books: divine transcendence (cf., e.g., Job 9:4 and Isa. 40:26, Job 9:8 and Isa. 44:24b, etc.); existence or being (cf., e.g., Job 4:19 and Isa. 45:9, 11); and the Servant of God (cf., e.g., Job 3:23 and Isa. 40:27a). He concludes that Job and Second Isaiah are related by language, style, and fundamental themes and that Second Isaiah is responding to the existential questions raised by Job. The question of dependence is clear for Terrien. Second Isaiah must be borrowing from Job and not vice versa. He believes it would be difficult to assume Job would not have utilized the prophet's notion of vicarious suffering and of *bara'*, to "create," if the prophet preceded the wisdom writer.

Whybray has studied the passage in Isaiah 40:12-14 carefully, focusing his concern on the precise meaning, intention, and setting for this text.[11]

> Who has measured the waters in the hollow of his hand
> and marked off the heavens with a span,
> enclosed the dust of the earth in a measure
> and weighed the mountains in scales
> and the hills in a balance?
> Who has directed the Spirit of the LORD,
> or as his counselor has instructed him?
> Whom did he consult for his enlightenment,
> and who taught him the path of justice,
> and taught him knowledge,
> and showed him the way of understanding?

Whybray does not believe there is direct wisdom influence in this text, but does find the influence of the court which he believes to be closely related. The wisdom and power of Yahweh are intended to be contrasted with "powerless and even nonexistent" Babylonian gods. If Whybray is correct, the continuity of Second Isaiah's proclamation of the wisdom of God with Isaiah of Jerusalem may be reflected in similar themes and motifs but is occasioned by an altogether different threat or debate. No longer are the wise in Israel the objects of this teaching, but rather the gods in Babylon to whom the exiles might have been drawn in view of the collapse of their own nation.

Finally, Ward has recently produced a study of a major dimension of Second Isaiah's thought, namely the knowledge of God.[12] While not maintaining dependence of the prophet upon any particular focus of the wisdom tradition, he traces many of the concerns of the prophet noted above, which are surely compatible with and parallel to much wisdom literature. Finally, he directs his attention to Isaiah 53:11 (one of two possible translations).

> Out of his mortal travail he shall see light and be satisfied;
> By his knowledge the righteous one, my servant,
> shall make many righteous and bear their iniquities.

He concludes that the knowledge of the servant is the knowledge of God and "the decisive factor in the eventual success of his life and work." Ultimately such a realization cannot be made by mere perception, but "includes knowledge, commitment, and faith."[13] Ward shows, therefore, that the elements of the wisdom tradition utilized by this prophet have been incorporated into a much larger whole which requires commitment and obedience to a creator God whose wisdom transcends that of finite man. Nevertheless, there is a need and call for at least this much discernment to make such commitment possible.

In concluding our study of the wisdom tradition as found in exilic non-wisdom sources, it must first be repeated that, understandably, there is little evidence of any institution or group which might provide the social setting for this tradition in this period. Ezekiel does point to the strong possibility that varieties of popular wisdom, transmitted perhaps by the elders, among others, were current. Second Isaiah may be responding to a royal wisdom, associated and identified with Babylonian gods.[14] We must also recognize the possibility that a Deuteronomic movement, strongly influenced by and in contact with the wisdom tradition as mediated partially through the scribes, was active in this period. Nevertheless, the exile is a time of fragmentation, of dreams, of lament, and to seek stable institutions in this period is inappropriate.

The wisdom found in Ezekiel, Second Isaiah, and perhaps Genesis 1 is being used by these sources to defend the notion of God's sovereignty and man's responsibility, and to provide the basis for both judgment and hope. The only wisdom literature most often associated with this period, Job, has many of these concerns. Regardless of the question of Second Isaiah's dependence upon Job, certain issues raised by the fall of Judah concerning both God and man are dealt with by prophet and sage. Moreover, the future development of the wisdom tradition in the post-exilic wisdom literature is probably influenced by both prophetic and wisdom responses to the exile. The dichotomies which will inevitably result in apocalyptic are, at this time, focused more on issues of the institutional basis for restoration than on ideological conflicts between the wise, the prophets, and the priests.[15] It is difficult to find firm indicators for who the wise are and where they may be located in this period. In any case, it would appear that the prophets themselves were carriers and shapers of this tradition. Perhaps there were no official wise men in the exile. Nevertheless, the teaching of wisdom and the literary forms used to express it lived on in the prophets Ezekiel and Second Isaiah, demonstrating a basic compatibility of worldview and perspective, an inadequate institutional base, and a willingness to address the hard questions posed at this time.

CHAPTER VII
WISDOM IN THE POST-EXILIC PERIOD

The wisdom tradition is usually thought of in connection with the period after the exile. Here it is associated with the establishment of a highly structured community centered around the cult, a new emphasis upon torah, the continuing absence of a monarchy, and the rise of the scribes to positions of power and influence. Most of the wisdom literature, at least in its final redacted form, is assigned to this period. The particular perspectives of wisdom which govern its final "development" are attributed to the sociological, theological, and historical characteristics of this period.

Once more, our focus in this period will not be upon the wisdom literature itself but upon the other forms of literature which reflect the influence of the wisdom tradition. In view of the many recent studies which suggest that much of the wisdom literature is pre-exilic, it is important to determine what can be ascertained from the non-wisdom traditions.

With the establishment of a hierarchical cultic power structure in post-exilic Israel, it is generally assumed that the scribes are much more closely attached to the cult—indeed, that most of them are priests. With the development of a "religion of the book," those who had special literary ability and knowledge of the traditions contained therein are said to take over progressively the functions usually and previously attached to the prophet and priest.[1] Too often this development is explained primarily on the basis of the necessary changes wrought by the exile, the waning of the prophets, the emphasis on exposition of the divine word, the new institutions made necessary by the times, etc. To this point our study would indicate that the interrelationship of the wisdom traditions with other traditions and the social settings associated with those who utilized it made it possible for the *sopherim* and other groups to fill the void left by the exilic experience. While there can be no doubt that the exile had tremendous repercussions for the future development of Israelite religion, the wisdom tradition had already demonstrated such an integral connection with the major prophetic, Deuteronomic, and other traditions that an important role in the theological and sociological response to the exile was virtually assured in the post-exilic period.

Post-exilic Prophecy

The post-exilic period contains much less prophetic literature than the pre-exilic and exilic periods. There are many explanations for this, but surely the separation of prophetic circles from the central locus of power is at least partially responsible.[2] The slight testimony to the wisdom tradition in these prophets may perhaps be explained analogously. That is, to the extent that the carriers of the wisdom tradition continue to be associated with the most powerful and "established" institutions in Israel and the prophets are further and further separated from them, the possibility of dialogue and confrontation becomes more difficult and the use and growth of the tradition less likely. Eventually the prophetic critique develops into apocalyptic (cf. below), and at that point we can see the wisdom tradition has not been totally absent. Although the chronological order of the post-exilic prophets is difficult to determine and often debated, we will attempt to present the evidence in as sequential an arrangement as possible.

Perhaps the first mention of the wisdom tradition is found in Obadiah 8:

> Will I not on that day, says the LORD,
>   destroy the wise men out of Edom,
>   and understanding out of Mount Esau?

This brief mention of the wise cannot stand the weight often placed upon it to explain and to prove the existence of an institutional form of wisdom in foreign countries surrounding Israel. Nevertheless, the exilic or early post-exilic prophet stands in line with First and Second Isaiah, among others, in juxtaposing the power and will of Yahweh against the "wisdom" of foreign nations. It therefore demonstrates a common theme which may perhaps be partially responsible for the future equation of wisdom and Yahweh in apocryphal wisdom literature.

It is interesting to note that the circle of Second Isaiah's followers usually associated with Isaiah 56–66 does not utilize the forms or content of the wisdom tradition to the extent of their leader/teacher. Among the few observations made are: two proverbial type passages which make their point with allusions to natural phenomena (61:11, 65:8); two passages focusing on the descendants of the land as the ones blessed by Yahweh; and the similarity of terminology between 65:1 and Prov. 1:28-31, and 66:1-2 and Prov. 9:1-6.[3] The fact that the prophetic circle's concerns have changed may be one reason why the wisdom tradition is not reflected more substantively.[4]

Some attempts have been made to suggest connections between wisdom and the prophets Haggai (2:5) and Zechariah (4:6, 5:2), but overall these comparisons do not aid us in delineating the shape of the wisdom tradition. A better case can be made for Malachi, however. The proverbial type saying in 1:6 is often seen as similar to wisdom sayings in form and content.

> "A son honors his father, and servant his master. If then I am a father, where is my honor? And if I am a master, where is my fear?"

A verse from chapter 2 aids us in ascertaining the development and locus for torah in the early post-exilic period.

> For the lips of a priest should guard knowledge, and men should seek instruction from his mouth, for he is the messenger of the LORD of hosts. (2:7)

If earlier hypotheses examined concerning the concept of torah are correct in locating it partially within the wisdom circles, then either the new priestly society has usurped this function or those charged with this function and responsibility have been fully integrated into this new societal structure.[5] Another passage, concerned with the polarity of righteous-wicked, theodicy, and a retributional framework for understanding Yahweh's judgment is Mal. 3:13–18.

> "Your words have been stout against me, says the LORD. Yet you say, 'How have we spoken against thee?' You have said, 'It is vain to serve God. What is the good of our keeping his charge or walking as in mourning before the LORD of hosts? Henceforth we deem the arrogant blessed; evildoers not only prosper but when they put God to the test they escape.'"
>
> Then those who feared the LORD spoke with one another; the LORD heeded and heard them, and a book of remembrance was written before him of those who feared the LORD and thought on his name. "They shall be mine, says the LORD of hosts, my special possession on the day when I act, and I will spare them as a man spares his son who serves him. Then once more you shall distinguish between the righteous and the wicked, between one who serves God and one who does not serve him."

Finally, if the disputation speeches of Second Isaiah have stylistic parallels with wisdom literature, and if the questioning of God's justice is a common concern of both prophet and wisdom tradition, then we have further formal and thematic elements which tie these two together more closely.[6]

Finally, we must examine evidence cited for the presence of the wisdom tradition in the Book of Jonah. The legendary nature of the book and its ostensible didactic character set it apart from the other prophetic books. Indeed, these differences alone create the possibility of a provenance for this book more closely associated with scribal and/or wisdom circles. Some have even labeled the book as an example of "wisdom-poetry."[7] The concern for creation (1:9), nature (2:1), knowledge (4:11), the confession in 4:2 (cf. Exod. 34:6f.) are among the thematic elements mentioned.[8] One of the most complete overviews of the evidence has been made by Trible, who notes the timeless nature of the message (general validity), the international scope, the use of natural phenomena, the lightness and humor, the informality of style, and some of the other evidence cited above. Trible's conclusion is that Jonah indeed reflects a sapiential milieu, perhaps to be found in the setting of the *sod*, the council or assembly, a place of informal gatherings often associated with the wisdom movement.[9]

When all of post-exilic prophecy is surveyed, the picture of the wisdom tradition achieved is not clear. On the one hand, there is surely evidence that the forms and message of wisdom continue to be used by the prophets. No longer, however, does the message of wisdom seem to be influential upon the prophets as in the past. Perhaps we must search for other arenas and circles within Israel at this time in order to find a closer interrelationship between the wise and Israelite religion.

Esther

The Book of Esther, not usually associated with any of the major Old Testament theological traditions, has been studied thoroughly by Talmon and designated a historicized wisdom tale.[10] He notes the familiarity of the author with "court etiquette and public administration," the presence of typical wisdom themes and precepts, ancient Near Eastern parallels (especially Ahiqar), and the similarity of "general trends and ideas . . . rather than . . . formal literary parallels." The book "portrays applied wisdom."[11] That is, the characters and general message of the book are intended to reflect the teaching of the wisdom tradition as it would and should be lived. Talmon seeks to demonstrate the validity of his observations through a careful literary examination of the book, focusing on the nature of the characters and the message intended to be set forth by the particular development of the story. Perhaps what is most valuable about this study is not the wisdom genre claimed but rather the interrelationships between the story of Esther and other Old Testament and ancient Near Eastern traditions usually not connected to it. The picture of wisdom which comes from this analysis touches many different parts of wisdom literature, although Talmon attempts to categorize the final product as most compatible with later "theological" wisdom. However, the social setting for this wisdom is difficult to determine if on the one hand it is Israelite and on the other hand it is to be associated with the Persian court. Such a court locus for the wise man is indeed more possible for the author of the Joseph Story, and it is not surprising that Talmon uses the thesis of von Rad to help legitimate his own.

The Psalms

There is, perhaps, no collection of writings outside the wisdom literature itself which contains so much evidence of wisdom literary forms and teachings as the Psalms. Individual "wisdom psalms" may be often and easily separated generically from the hymns and laments which surround them. In their final canonical form, however, it is clear these particular psalms have been integrated into the cultic worship and life of Israel. Therefore, regardless of whether or not these psalms with wisdom characteristics testify to an active part by the wise in psalmody, it is clear that the Psalter witnesses to an interrelationship between the wisdom tradition and the cult, an interrelationship which must be taken seriously. Our analysis of the wisdom tradition's relationship to and use by proponents of other traditions make it doubtful that a clear separation of these traditions can or should be made.

A significant proportion of the psalms has been dated in the pre-exilic or exilic periods, including some of the wisdom psalms.[12] Some explanation of why the relationship of wisdom and the psalms is dealt with in the post-exilic period is therefore in order. First, the dating of most psalms is difficult, and there is little consensus about which psalms are actually pre-exilic. Nevertheless, it is clear that the psalms can no longer be viewed as the creation and song book of the Second Temple community. Even if it were possible to separate clearly the pre-exilic wisdom psalms and wisdom-influenced psalms from those originating in a later period, the conclusions reached would simply be further confirmation of an interrelationship between wisdom and the cult which has been suggested already. However, most wisdom psalms are dated in the post-exilic period and this is compatible with widely held views of the wisdom tradition, namely that in this period the wise became more and more involved in the established and central institution of Israel, the cult. More importantly, the Psalms *as a whole* reflect the needs and concerns of the post-exilic community and therefore tell us more about the wisdom tradition in this period than any other.

Research on wisdom in the Psalms has been relatively sparse when compared to the study expended on hymns and laments. Nevertheless, several studies of the characteristics of wisdom psalms have been completed, and many theories about the relationship between wisdom and cult propounded.[13] Unlike the lament or hymn of praise, there is no generic form or structure shared by a majority of wisdom psalms, although certain groups of wisdom psalms have some generic similarity (e.g., proverb poems, 'ashre poems, etc.). The general classification of "wisdom psalm" is made on the basis of rhetorical characteristics, particular wisdom forms found within the larger psalm (e.g., proverbs), and the presence of motifs, themes, and vocabulary usually identified with the theological concerns and perspectives of the wise. There are also a number of psalms which are not classified as wisdom psalms but which contain some of the same characteristics and therefore also

witness to an interrelationship between wisdom and cult. Before an
analysis of the implications of the presence of wisdom in the Psalms
occurs, a few illustrations are in order.

The following literary forms and styles, among others found
within the Psalms, have been identified with the wisdom tradition.

Admonition Put no confidence in extortion,
set no vain hopes on robbery;
if riches increase, set not your heart on them. (62:10)

'ashre
formula Blessed is the man who makes
the Lord his trust,
who does not turn to the proud,
to those who go astray after false gods! (40:4)

Numerical
Formula Once God has spoken;
twice have I heard this:
that power belongs to God;
and that to thee, O Lord, belongs steadfast love.
For thou dost requite a man
according to his work. (62:11-12)

"Better"
Saying Better is a little that the righteous has
than the abundance of many wicked. (37:16)

Rhetorical
Question Why should I fear in times of trouble,
when the iniquity of my persecutors surrounds me,
men who trust in their wealth
and boast of the abundance of their riches? (49:5-6)

Lists Cf. Ps. 104:14ff.

Proverbs The wicked plots against the righteous,
and gnashes his teeth at him;
but the Lord laughs at the wicked,
for he sees that his day is coming. (37:12-13)

Teacher's
Opening
Formula Give ear, O my people, to my teaching;
incline your ears to the words of my mouth!
I will open my mouth in a parable;
I will utter dark sayings from of old,
things that we have heard and known,
that our fathers have told us.
We will not hide them from their children,

> but tell to the coming generation
> the glorious deeds of the LORD, and his might,
> and the wonders which he has wrought.
> (78:1-4)

In addition to and in conjunction with these literary styles and forms, many psalms deal with themes and motifs common to wisdom literature such as the fear of the LORD (111:10), torah (119), retributional theology and the polarity of the wicked and righteous (1, 37, etc.), and theodicy (73). Although there is no consensus as to which psalms should be regarded as wisdom psalms, with few exceptions most scholars consider certain psalms best classified by this categorization (cf., e.g., Pss. 1, 37, 49, 112, 127, 128, among others). The virtual universal agreement that Psalm 1 is a wisdom psalm is quite significant,[14] for it provides an important framework for understanding the Psalter as a whole.

> Blessed is the man
>   who walks not in the counsel of the wicked,
> nor stands in the way of sinners,
>   nor sits in the seat of scoffers;
> but his delight is in the law of the LORD,
>   and on his law he meditates day and night.
> He is like a tree
>   planted by streams of water,
> that yields its fruit in its season,
>   and its leaf does not wither.
> In all that he does, he prospers.
>
> The wicked are not so,
>   but are like chaff which the wind drives away.
> Therefore the wicked will not stand in the judgment,
>   nor sinners in the congregation of the righteous;
> for the LORD knows the way of the righteous,
>   but the way of the wicked will perish.

What are the implications for our picture of the wisdom tradition in the post-exilic period on the basis of so many psalms which reflect either the authorship of the wise or at least integration of wisdom literary forms and message into psalms traditionally associated with a cultic provenance? Theologically there are two extremes, represented by the positions of Perdue and Mowinckel, among others. For Purdue, the wisdom writers did indeed have cultic concerns from an early period and actually composed poetry for the cult.[15] For Mowinckel, the wisdom psalms represent a very late stage of psalmody and with their emphasis on a wisdom piety and instruction incompatible with the more inclusive, communal (and normative) perspectives of the cult, reflect a disintegration of the psalm forms and theology.[16] With either of these positions or several which stand somewhere in between them, it is difficult to provide a concrete picture of the social setting of the wisdom tradition which would aid us in determining the validity of the positions taken.

At this point, perhaps a question sometimes asked of individual psalms but rarely of the wisdom psalms as a literary whole might help to shed more light on the question of setting. In light of the concern of many wisdom psalms with retribution theology, the two ways, the wicked and the righteous: "Who are the wicked"? Surely one answer to this question would be to dismiss it as being naïve and incapable of being answered in any concrete way. But it is precisely the concrete and general concern on the part of many wisdom psalms with the wicked, with an affirmation of God's presence with the righteous in spite of apparent evidence and experience to the contrary, which provides a possible answer. By and large, the enemy is viewed corporately (Pss. 1:6, 32:10, 34:16; 37:1, etc.). The psalmist is usually directing his testimony to the cultic community which, like him, is seeing with its own eyes the triumph of the wicked. Surely such a situation could be appropriate at any time in the post-exilic period, but we may still learn something about the rationale and occasion which might prompt such a psalm, or at least create a receptivity of theme and perspective. Compatibility of a cultic, corporate concern in such a post-exilic community with the situation presupposed by these wisdom psalms is also established.

The psalms do not have to be seen as the musings of wise men who, because they had control over the transmission of sacred tradition, chose to cast their pearls. The recent attempt by Crenshaw to locate wisdom's use of creation theology in a concern by the wise for divine justice is quite compatible with the motivation and situation which may lie behind the wisdom psalms.[17]

The wisdom psalms have been described as an example of the disintegration of the classical forms of psalmody. At the same time the similarities between wisdom psalms and the individual thanks-giving, the hymn, and other forms have been noted. It would appear that the new situation in which Israel found itself in the post-exilic period and the necessity of addressing questions of the prosperity of the wicked from perspectives found in another tradition, namely wisdom, would create the possibility for genre changes which should not be viewed as disintegration or dissolution but rather necessary transformation in the light of new circumstances. Such a view is attempting to take seriously both the setting of wisdom and the cult, rather than assuming that the former is responsible for a variant (and often perceived to be inferior) form and setting.

That a didactic intention is associated with wisdom psalms is almost universally accepted. Gerstenberger is representative of this perspective when he states: "Instruction in fact can be surmised to be the driving force behind most of the wisdom psalms."[18] In light of the proposal concerning the setting, it would appear wisdom psalms might also have another intention: to affirm the order of the world by a theology of retribution. The citation of various sentences (and the use of other wisdom literary conventions) drawing on experience, not necessarily that of the poet or community, is a common means to this end. Again, if we assume a community which has firsthand experience which contradicts at points the tenets of a theology of retribution, then it seems plausible to assume the wisdom sayings in these psalms intend to do more than teach; they need to comfort, to protest, to assure, to affirm the presence of God's loving kindness. In doing so the didactic nature of the individual elements is transformed as the appeal is transmitted through the cultic, corporate medium.

A few final observations about the nature of the relationship between wisdom and cult must be made. It has often been noted that the Israelite temple grew more and more individualistically oriented in the post-exilic period, the focus on the torah and adherence to it providing a natural connection with retribution theology. We have already seen such connections in other non-wisdom literature, particularly that influenced by the Deuteronomic movement. This development provides both the occasion and the rationale for the use of wisdom in this period. That is, the individualistic expressions in wisdom literature would appeal to the torah-oriented community, while at the same time the communal emphasis or presuppositions of cultic forms would ensure an easy transition and platform into the cultic community. The setting and intention of wisdom psalms as suggested above would be compatible with such a proposal. The combination of wisdom concerns and psalm forms, which could be used in cultic worship, would place individualism in its proper perspective. Once more, it is also clear that the great majority of non-wisdom traditions in the pre-exilic and exilic periods have utilized a wisdom tradition which had interests and concerns which transcended the individual, making such a suggested development more probable. It also warns us not to characterize the nature of the wisdom tradition solely by the forms and concerns found in the pre-exilic wisdom tradition.

The gradual development which makes possible the ultimate identification of the torah with wisdom has been discussed above, and the wisdom psalms seem to represent a further stage in this process. Would not an occasion appropriate to the development and presentation of retribution theology for the community through the wisdom psalms be a powerful stimulus and important component in this process? The use of torah by Isaiah, emphasizing instructional dimensions of wisdom and the fact that Yahweh is the teacher, coupled with the Deuteronomic use of the torah to explain the vicissitudes of Israel's history, are naturally developed by the cult as it seeks to understand its present situation.[19]

Finally, the use and transformation of various genres and subgenres of particular psalms (hymn, individual thanksgiving, etc.) reflected by the presence of wisdom psalms would seem to blunt a radical application of Mowinckel's thesis concerning wisdom psalms. The compatibility of cult and wisdom, gradually being asserted by Perdue and others, is a valid criterion for rejecting the pejorative view of late non-cultic psalmody as described by Mowinckel. Moreover, that compatibility, already witnessed to in previous chapters, also strengthens the stances of those who wish to see wisdom psalmody in an unbroken line of tradition rather than as the imposition of later styles and perspectives which ultimately result in disintegrated and inferior psalms.

Apocalyptic

Many different types of arguments have been made which in one way or another relate apocalyptic literature to the wisdom tradition. Most of the studies focus on the Book of Daniel. It is important to note, however, that the implications of a connection between apocalyptic and wisdom are much debated and far from clear.

The first six chapters of Daniel especially utilize the vocabulary of the wisdom tradition and develop themes which are common to it.

> And in every matter of wisdom and understanding concerning which the king inquired of them, he found them ten times better than all the magicians and enchanters that were in all his kingdom. (1:20)

> He changes times and seasons;
>   he removes kings and sets up kings;
> he gives wisdom to the wise
>   and knowledge to those who have understanding. (2:21)

> There is in your kingdom a man in whom is the spirit of the holy gods. In the days of your father light and understanding and wisdom, like the wisdom of the gods, were found in him, and King

> Nebuchadnezzar, your father, made him chief of the magicians, enchanters, Chaldeans, and astrologers, because an excellent spirit, knowledge, and understanding to interpret dreams, explain riddles, and solve problems were found in this Daniel. . . . (5:11-12)
>
> When I, Daniel, had seen the vision, I sought to understand it. . . . (8:15)
>
> And he understood the word and had understanding of the vision. (10:1)

The parallels between these passages and the Joseph Story have long been noted. In both stories the hero is an interpreter of dreams, a man possessing wisdom, close to the court, an advisor of kings. In Daniel, however, the wisdom of God is developed in a way much more reminiscent of Job, Qoheleth, and First and Second Isaiah. Thus while the concern of the Book of Daniel with wisdom can scarcely be denied, the character of that wisdom has changed significantly. Partially, this change would seem a response to a critique and subsequent use and development by the prophets.

Von Rad and Whybray, among others, have suggested that the parallels between wisdom and Daniel indicate that wisdom is the mother of apocalyptic rather than prophecy, the more usual phenomenon from which apocalyptic is seen to originate.[20] The most powerful argument used in drawing this conclusion notes the disparity between the views of history found in most major Old Testament traditions and apocalyptic—between a focus on the "fluidity" versus the "unalterable nature" of historical events. The wisdom tradition's notion of the "appropriate time" is seen to be much closer to the later, deterministic notion of history.[21] Compare, for example, the following wisdom and apocalyptic passages.

Blessed be the name of God for ever and ever, to whom belong wisdom and might.	For everything there is a season, and a time for every matter under heaven;
He changes times and seasons; he removes kings and sets up kings;	a time to be born, and a time to die. . . . (Eccles. 3:1-2)

he gives wisdom to the wise and knowledge to those who have understanding;
he reveals deep and mysterious things.
he knows what is in the darkness, and the light dwells with him.
To thee, O God of my fathers, I give thanks and praise, for thou hast given me wisdom and strength,
and hast now made known to me what we asked of thee,
for thou hast made known to us the king's matter. (Dan. 2:20-23)

Before the universe was created, it was known to him;
so it was also after it was finished. (Ben Sira 23:20)

The works of the Lord are all good, and he will supply every need in its hour.
And no one can say, "This is worse than that,"
for all things will prove good in their season.
So now sing praise with all your heart and voice,
and bless the name of the Lord. (Ben Sira 39:33-34)

Although the theory of von Rad that the origin of apocalyptic is to be located in wisdom tradition has not met with widespread approval, the interrelationship of wisdom and apocalyptic should not be immediately dismissed. Surely the Book of Daniel and other apocalyptic material reflects the use of wisdom by apocalyptic circles. The members of these circles are in all probability those who feel a threat to their communal identity and goals from outside sources (e.g., Hellenism) or who have in some way been disenfranchised by those within their own community who have maintained some authority, often by accepting the structures imposed upon them from outside powers. Not only the integrity of particular religious traditions and practices are at stake for such apocalyptic circles, but variant conceptions of God, the way he makes himself known, the nature of his world, and other important conceptions are at issue. Hanson has shown that the beginnings of apocalyptic eschatology may be found as early as Isaiah 56–66 in the conflicting hopes for a new society with followers of Ezekiel and others,[22] and the resultant disappointment and disillusionment of

Second Isaiah's followers. It is not at all surprising or inconceivable that the followers of the prophets, who are at least partially responsible for apocalyptic, would utilize the prophetic interpretation of God as the source of wisdom. Moreover, they might well connect themselves, as visionaries, with the source of special knowledge concerning the final end of this age, a time when the injustice of this age, as seen in the religious practices of both foreigners and Israelites, will be destroyed.

Despite this connection of the wisdom tradition to both the antecedent prophetic and contemporary apocalyptic voices, it is difficult to maintain with von Rad the view of "the apocalyptist as wise man."[23] Surely the wisdom tradition can and must be related to apocalyptic, but the locus and vehicle for its transmission is the prophetic tradition and the circles which kept it alive—in all probability these were not the wise. The evidence of the post-exilic literature, particularly the Psalms, indicates another locus for the major carriers of the wisdom tradition of this period, associated as we have come to expect, with the center of power, the establishment, the cult.

Many theories abound concerning the shape and nature of the wisdom tradition in the post-exilic period, most of them based upon the wisdom literature itself. The evidence from the non-wisdom traditions of this period do not aid us significantly in confirming any theories of schools for the well-to-do, scribal apprentices, etc. Nevertheless, both prophetic and apocalyptic material witness to a continuation and development of the uses of wisdom in the pre-exilic and exilic periods by the prophets. More importantly the growth of the focus on torah as instruction, as the will of Yahweh to be obeyed (cf. Deuteronomy), is reflected in the Psalms. While the distinctions made by Gordis and others concerning the potential social settings for wisdom do not seem verifiable by the existing evidence, a close connection between the wisdom tradition and the cult is indicated.[24] Not only are the wise now charged with responsibility for the torah, but they are also involved in relating their retributional theological perspectives to the questions of theodicy now raised by the absence of previous signs of Israel's election. Their theological message is also now applied to those within the community itself who violate the mandates established by the cult to ensure Yahweh's favor. In one sense the wisdom tradition can be seen to have once more gravitated to the locus of power and used its considerable skill and perception to maintain its authority. In another sense, however, the wisdom tradition has itself been a transforming agent, focusing the community's attention on the hard questions of life and existence it now faces and providing it with a structure and rationale for understanding the action and love of Yahweh—torah.

CHAPTER VIII
CONCLUSIONS

Summary and Synthesis

The two primary purposes of our study to this point have been:
(1) to examine in a roughly chronological sequence the extent and
character of the wisdom tradition in non-wisdom literature as
designated by contemporary scholarship; and (2) to make a
preliminary attempt to trace the development of the wisdom
tradition itself as it is found and used in these other traditions. It is
clear from the outset that any comments about wisdom must be
referential in character, for the primary texts and traditions
examined are not wisdom literature, and at best can only point
toward the wisdom tradition and its theology and social locus. In
this sense our investigation has focused more on the character of
non-wisdom literature rather than on the wisdom literature.

In spite of this observation, there is no doubt that certain aspects
of Old Testament non-wisdom literature are compared most
profitably with the literary forms and theological concerns most
often identiifed with the wisdom literature itself. Though few if any
scholars would agree that all the textual material cited and
examined above should be connected to the wisdom tradition, no
one would deny that certain comparisons (and with them
subsequent suppositions about "influence" or a common shared

intellectual tradition) are appropriate and important. What is perhaps most significant for the present study is not the validity of any particular assertion made about, for example, the Succession Narrative, the Joseph Story, Amos, or Daniel, but rather the theological nature of the non-wisdom traditions which have been compared with wisdom. However the wisdom tradition is defined on the basis of its use and occurrence in Old Testament literature, there seems to be no doubt it was an important element in the message of the whole. Further, its particular perspectives cannot be merely attributed to later redactors (cf. below).

It is the purpose of this final chapter to begin to define more precisely the nature of the wisdom tradition in light of the textual witnesses examined above; to compare the message and development of the wisdom tradition as found in non-wisdom literature to current theories based primarily on wisdom literature alone; and finally to examine some of the implications of our conclusions for future study of the Old Testament and its use in contemporary theology. Before we attempt to determine the nature of the wisdom tradition, however, a summary of the observations made to this point is in order.

The non-wisdom literature of the Old Testament reflects the existence of a popular aphoristic wisdom, often expressed in oral and literary forms traditionally associated with wisdom literature throughout the ancient Near East. This popular wisdom seems to be present from the beginning of Israel's occupation of Palestine and continues to be used in a variety of ways throughout the periods we have examined (cf., e.g., Ezekiel). While the evidence for a clan or family origin for wisdom in the pre-monarchical period is sparse, the supposition that this was an important locus and means of transmission for early wisdom is strengthened by an examination of motive clauses in early legal material,[1] the didactic functions of the existent examples of this wisdom (perhaps to be connected to familial [father-son] authority structures), and the ostensible absence of other major institutional carriers for this wisdom. This

Conclusions   139

popular wisdom soon becomes detached from its "roots," whatever
they may have been, and is utilized in a number of ways, often
different from their original intention. In this separation, these
forms and teachings are often attached to the concerns of
institutions, usually in a later period, quite different from those of
their origin (cf., e.g., Judg. 9:8-15). The multiplicity of settings and
uses of popular wisdom, regardless of its origin and initial means of
transmission, witnesses to a certain commonness and sharing of this
type of thinking and style of expression. This makes a precise
determination of social setting difficult.

When the literature usually associated with the early monarchical period is examined, certain changes can be seen to have occurred
which no longer allow us to speak primarily in terms of popular
wisdom. Not only have the theological characteristics and concerns
of wisdom changed to a certain degree, but the sources in which
wisdom is found are closely aligned with one particular institution,
namely the monarchy. It is possible to select passages dealing with
particular monarchical officials which witness to "secular" perspectives on the part of those officials.[2] Nevertheless, when viewed
as a whole the use of the wisdom tradition in the early monarchy
does not suggest a definition of wisdom as "secular empiricism" in
this period.[3] The wisdom tradition is instead integrally tied to the
major Yahwistic traditions of the time, and is utilized to speak of
creation (Gen. 2–3) and the wisdom of Yahweh (1 Kings 3-11), as
well as the Yahwistic authority behind the monarchy (1 Kings 3-11,
Succession Narrative) and its officials (Joseph Story).

The monarchical period witnesses to a connection between the
wisdom tradition and institutional sources of power. We have noted
that one use of wisdom tended to be to legitimate monarchical
structures and personnel. Surely von Rad is correct in seeing at least
one motivation for this, namely that wisdom teaching itself was in
need of legitimation.[4] Such an observation clearly has implications
for the social setting of this tradition, but it has theological
implications as well. That is, from the outset, intentionally or not,

the wisdom tradition is tied closely to the major Yahwistic interpretations of Israel's history. Therefore it has a stake in these particular perspectives and the institutions which stand or fall with them. This does not necessarily presuppose "nationalization" of wisdom at this time, but it does posit a basic compatibility of national or monarchical concerns, at both institutional and conceptual (ideological) levels, which makes later developments in the tradition seem more continuous and less of a break from the past.

In the later monarchical period both the prophets and the Dueteronomic movement make use of and at the same time influence the wisdom tradition. Amos, perhaps Micah, and Ezekiel utilize popular wisdom, some of which may have had its origin in the clan, to proclaim their message to the people. It is important to recognize that *all* the forms and terminology associated with wisdom in the prophets (except, perhaps, the woe oracles) have parallels in wisdom literature itself, thus witnessing to a common literary tradition for those forms regardless of the different origins and means of transmission wisdom may have had. Jeremiah and particularly Isaiah of Jerusalem appear to call into question the allegiance of those who utilize wisdom to legitimate monarchical structures and ideology. The focus and emphasis on Yahweh as the sole source of wisdom, the role of the prophet and Yahweh's anointed as counselor, and the function of torah demonstrate this concern, even conflict, with those who have in some way utilized wisdom to authorize monarchical perspectives in a one-sided manner.

Even the prophets who attack the misuse of wisdom utilize its forms and teachings in a way which reflects a positive attitude toward its message. The Deuteronomic movement, influenced no doubt by earlier prophets, attempts to use the wisdom tradition in a reform of monarchy and cult. Surely the doctrine of rewards, the fear of the Lord, and humanistic concerns cannot be attributed solely to the wisdom tradition.[5] Nevertheless, Weinfeld and others have made a convincing case for the presence, even influence, of a scribal circle associated with such teaching in the composition of the Deuteronomic literature.

In the exile the institutional bases most commonly associated with the wisdom tradition disappear. In spite of this, concerns which reflect the continued importance and use of wisdom are found, especially in Ezekiel and Isaiah 40–55. The connection of wisdom with creation in Second Isaiah is especially significant in view of parallels with Job and its partial function of asserting that Yahweh is responsible for all things. This conception, when applied to the question of theodicy, so often raised in the exilic and post-exilic periods, can result in a disparity between present and future expectations which may have led to apocalpytic. The theological moralism and dualism which is found in apocalyptic can also be associated with wisdom's "two ways." Finally, the presence of wisdom in the Psalter reflects the use of this tradition in conjunction with the institutional power base for the post-exilic period, the cult. In view of previous associations with such authoritative bases, as well as a fundamental compatibility with other major Yahwistic traditions, this is hardly surprising.

The Social Setting of Wisdom

Throughout this study we have continually noted that the evidence provided by non-wisdom literature which would lead to a clearer picture of the social setting of the wisdom tradition itself has simply not been present. This is not surprising. The authors of most biblical literature were not sages; therefore the present setting of these texts will not be reflective of the wisdom tradition, but will be, at most, simply one compatible with this tradition. The question of "schools" for the wise connected to the court remains open on the basis of this study, though this or a similar setting is attractive for other reasons (proverbial composition and collection, ancient Near Eastern parallels, etc.).

One important affirmation about the social setting of wisdom is made by our study. Kovacs, Clements, Moore, Heaton and others have suggested that leaders, scribes, administrative officials, and others connected to the court are to be associated with the wisdom tradition. In view of an association with the monarchy as a locus of power found in non-wisdom literature, such a hypothesis is attractive. Von Rad, who stresses the need for legitimation on the part of the wise, does not believe the non-wisdom narrative works reflect this need. If only the theological perspectives governing the whole are examined, this may be true. However, it appears that the institutions which motivate and create such narratives are legitimated by them and that the officials of such institutions are rather closely associated with the positive or negative results of such attempts at legitimation. This makes it probable that the overall intention of such works can be used to locate at least part of the wisdom tradition sociologically. We can therefore agree with Murphy and others who maintain the wisdom tradition had popular and royal origins and that the majority of its literature is most probably associated with the latter. The precise shape of the institutions which may have been existent for transmission of and training in wisdom continues to elude us.[6]

The Development of the Wisdom Tradition

If the forms and message of the wisdom tradition as utilized by non-wisdom literature are borrowed either directly or indirectly from circles ultimately responsible for the wisdom literature itself, then we should expect a chronological correlation between the developments found in each literary corpus. This correlation or compatibility may not, however, be seen only in terms of parallel usage. It would also appear in terms of the growth and change effected by the influence of the different traditions and perspectives on one another. In the brief comparative analysis which follows, our goal is not to critique traditional theories of the development of wisdom but rather to understand how a holistic overview of the use of wisdom by non-wisdom traditions can define more fully the nature and development of the wisdom tradition. Implicit in this study is the belief that the growth and development of any tradition is best determined not simply by an examination of the material devoted solely to that tradition's peculiar points of view, but by investigating the interrelationships between a particular tradition and others which also have an important role in its overall development.

It has long been maintained that the prophetic movement in particular had a great effect upon the future growth and development of the wisdom tradition. Recent studies of the use of wisdom in the prophets would confirm such a view.[7] An examination of the use of wisdom throughout the Old Testament would broaden such a position, however, by maintaining that it was not the prophets alone, but many different traditions which entered into dialogue with or utilized the teachings of wisdom and subsequently affected its development. An underlying presupposition for some who maintain prophetic influence upon wisdom has been that in this period wisdom finally begins to "see the light," to understand the theological dimensions of a previously secular and empirical wisdom, to take more seriously the nationalistic character of "true" Israelite religion (election, torah, etc.). This eventually culminates in the teaching of someone like Ben Sira. Such a presupposition is not affirmed by the non-wisdom literature, which integrally related wisdom and its teachings to major theological and national concerns from the early monarchy on. It is difficult to believe this could have been the case if the wisdom tradition considered itself dramatically different from other religious traditions. Moreover, the probable close association of wisdom and those institutions responsible for the creation and transmission of the fundamental theological traditions makes this presupposition more problematic.

At this point a brief overview of theories of the theological development found in wisdom literature itself is in order. By and large, commentators on this development share one basic tenet: that wisdom gradually becomes more theological and nationalistic in orientation throughout the history of Israelite religion. The illustrations cited and reasons given for such a development are rarely the same, but such a progressive development remains common to most. The basic differences in this general view have to do with the character of wisdom at the starting point, usually the monarchy, the number of "stages" involved (and their causes), and the distinct nature of wisdom at any particular point during its development. For many, wisdom is initially secular, anthropocentric, even non-Yahwistic, in its message, often under the direct or indirect influence of Egyptian wisdom.[8] For others, wisdom is Yahwistic from the beginning, though this does not necessarily mean religious or theological. Indeed, "secular" is often used to describe this early Yahwistic wisdom.[9]

Coupled with these theories of theological development are further theories concerning the transmitters of the tradition. For example, Scott posits a development from folk wisdom to family to school to counselors to scribes.[10] Moore, Weinfeld, and others have nuanced this development in recent studies, while others (Whybray, etc.) have refused to posit such theories in view of the paucity of the evidence.[11]

What contribution does a study of non-wisdom literature make to a theory of the development of the wisdom tradition? In view of the studies of Gerstenberger, Wolff, and others, it would seem that any theory which posits an absorption of popular wisdom into a more stylized, court wisdom in the early monarchy must be modified in at least two ways. First, Amos and Ezekiel witness to the existence of popular wisdom forms and message in a non-court setting which had not yet been (totally) absorbed into court wisdom, although parallels in style and content make clear that certain literary forms belong at the court as well. Second, on the basis of wisdom forms attached to a clan/popular setting found in Amos and elsewhere, it is difficult to assume a progressive development in wisdom literature and style. Whatever factors are involved in a thesis which maintains an increasing literary sophistication from popular to court wisdom need to be rethought in light of studies of non-wisdom literature.

The evidence available confirms the view of those who maintain that Israelite wisdom, as it has been passed down to us in wisdom and non-wisdom literature, was thoroughly Yahwistic. This does not deny the gradually increasing focus on Yahweh as the source of wisdom and the progressive inclusion of important elements of salvation history traditions within later wisdom literature. The empirical nature of proverbial teachings concerned primarily with domestic affairs in "earlier" sayings is not denied, either. However, all of these sayings are concerned from the beginning to legitimate themselves on the basis of a Yahwistic umbrella, one which took seriously the ideologies associated with other traditions, especially those associated with the monarchy.

Although there can be no doubt that wisdom progressively became more involved in "God-talk," the use of the wisdom tradition in non-wisdom literature warns us against assuming too quicky or facilely a development from "empirical to theological," "secular to religious/theological," etc. Crenshaw has described the growth and development of the wisdom tradition in terms of a "process of theologization."[12] The evidence we have examined would confirm this. From the outset the wisdom tradition was theological in concern and character. This involves more than the assumption of a theological or Yahwistic framework for early Israelite wisdom. Rather, in view of the connection of the tradition with creation (though we recognize the anthropocentric focus of Gen. 2–3), sacral law, and the Yahwistic foundations for the early monarchy and its history, any theory which posits concerns with these elements as "new" in a later, more theologically oriented period is difficult to accept. The picture of Israelite religion gained by an examination of the wisdom tradition in non-wisdom literature reflects not simply an interrelationship with the carriers of these traditions, but a mutual interest in the theological framework which provides Israel with identity. When particular themes, motifs, and concerns of the wisdom tradition are examined, for example torah, the fear of the Lord, or theodicy, one finds theological development to be sure. But such development is dependent upon the history and growth of all Israelite religious traditions, their interrelationship, and mutual, reciprocal influence. It is to this dimension of the wisdom tradition we now turn.

Wisdom and Tradition

What kind of a relationship between the wisdom tradition and other traditions is indicated by this study? We have already observed that our evidence is inferential in nature, for in no instance can we be certain of a *direct* contribution by the wise to the non-wisdom traditions. Moreover, the intermix of wisdom and non-wisdom, and the virtual certainty that much of the wisdom thought borrowed was at least one step removed from its oral and literary provenance and now part of a common cultural stock does not make our task easier. Nevertheless, the basic presupposition and first step in determining the interrelationship of wisdom with other traditions would appear to be possible, namely, the separation, the distinguishing of wisdom from other perspectives. In making this first step we have rejected the notion that wisdom was simply a part of a common religious tradition, for such an amorphous description does not explain adequately the relationship between wisdom and the prophets witnessed to by the biblical texts, to cite just one example. We would therefore agree with von Rad, Clements, Crenshaw, and others that boundaries are needed, though Murphy is also correct to stress a common understanding of reality lying behind the distinctive religious traditions of Israel.

Two more points need to be stressed here. First, in order to distinguish or find the wisdom tradition in non-wisdom traditions we are necessarily dependent upon wisdom literature as reflective of both the source and means of transmission for this tradition initially. We do not pretend to escape the critique of circular reasoning by Crenshaw and others here, but we would maintain that this type of reasoning is not only necessary, it is indicative of the process by which the wisdom tradition transmits itself to Israelite culture and is subsequently influenced by the culture's appropriation and interpretation of it! Second, in distinguishing wisdom from other traditions it is not necessary to assume that our contemporary epistemological and theological perspectives are operative in Israelite culture. These particular distinctions, as developed in the past, not only dichotomize or polarize these traditions, they make it difficult to understand how wisdom can be found in so many different contexts.

In rejecting both a common religious tradition and the polarities of reason-revelation, nature-history, etc., as adequately characterizing the relationship of wisdom to other Old Testament traditions, we need another conceptual model to explain this relationship. We would hope that this model will stem from the sociological (to the extent it can be determined) and theological evidence provided by the Old Testament itself. We would suggest a pluralistic model, similar to those set forth by Hanson in his study of early apocalyptic and Bauer in his work on early Christianity.[13] A pluralistic matrix best explains the growth and development of Israelite religion, for it automatically relativizes the polarities between traditions while at the same time recognizing differences with regard to social setting and theological stance. The peculiarly Israelite and Yahwistic understanding of reality, informed by a belief in Yahweh's presence, concern, and actions in the world, governs and frames all traditions. Within such an understanding are to be found several different, sometimes competing and conflicting, traditions. These traditions have their own particular perspectives and interpretation of how one perceives and articulates this understanding, as well as their own social bases. The Old Testament itself is a microcosm of such a pluralistic society, reflecting both the commonness and the diversity found within it.

What is important to emphasize, however, is that the mixture of traditions found within any particular Old Testament source is not simply demonstrative of a final synthesis. Rather, to the extent that one can posit many different traditions contemporary with each other, it is reflective of an interrelationship, a borrowing, a utilization of one tradition by another and the subsequent growth and continued interchange between them. Surely there will be occasions when certain theological traditions will be firmly attached to institutional power, and it is at those times when a monolithic-or-thodox perspective, the property of one particular group, threatens to disenfranchise other traditions, to cut them off from a means by which their perspectives may be made known. Even at these times, however, the biblical witness reflects continuation of fundamental traditions and perspectives, though often only set forth by later movements after a change in institutional power has occurred (cf., e.g. the northern Levitical traditions in Deuteronomy).

We have noted the peculiar tendency of the wisdom tradition to gravitate toward the locus of institutional power, utilizing its anthropocentric (the monarchy) or theocentric (the cult) ideological perspectives to legitimate both itself and the institution. This demonstrates an important aspect of the wisdom tradition: that wisdom's propensity to find, define, and delineate the "order" of the natural world will often and most frequently associate itself with the institutions responsible for that order in society. There are surely occasions when wisdom can and has been used by those who critique the present order who believe their own, usually distinctive, even esoteric (contrasted with those whose "order" they critique) wisdom provides different, but nonetheless valid, conceptions of Israel's history and future. These are the visionaries, the dreamers, the disenfranchised. The wisdom tradition, even in the post-exilic period, was never the major or sole defender of the institutions in power, but was always found in combination or conjunction with other major traditions tied to the same locus. Thus, whether in times of relative stability and free interchange among many traditions, or in times of movements toward orthodoxy and subsequent silencing of dissenting voices, the fact that the wisdom tradition is often a part of the "orthodox" response means that never is pluralism totally lost. It continues on an ideological level, even though it may appear diminished socially and institutionally. It is precisely this constant use of many traditions, even in the most oppressive of times, that creates anew the possibilities of reform and change, for these possibilities are latent in the traditions themselves. Moreover, the wisdom tradition is always there, ready to legitimate, and at the same time to critique, those who argue for change. We have seen, however, that this mix of traditions continually provides new perspectives, new opportunities for growth, making it possible for wisdom not simply to call for reestablishment of the old, but to learn from past critiques by other traditions and to utilize these in the building of a new order.

We would suggest that any model which attempts to take seriously the pluralistic nature of Israelite society must first distinguish the traditions involved and at the same time recognize their constant interrelationship with each other.[14] This interrelationship is not the result of a theoretical model aimed at providing the most possibilities for dialogue and growth; it is rather a necessary assumption if we are to explain adequately the presence of the wisdom tradition in non-wisdom literature.

Finally, we should note one other way in which wisdom has been related to other Old Testament traditions. Recently Sheppard has examined the final verses of Qoheleth and concluded that they represent a redactional perspective, influenced by Sirach, which has as its purpose "to include it fully within a 'canon conscious' definition of sacred wisdom, one that is remarkably similar to that of Sirach and Baruch."[15] Likewise, "Psalm 1 provides a redactional preface to the Psalter. . . . The Psalter thus becomes a source book for such a reading of the Torah as wisdom, a guide to the obedient life.''[16] The approach of Sheppard, influenced by the stress on a canonical interpretation of Scripture of his teacher, Childs, has made an important contribution to our overall theological evaluation of wisdom and the entire Old Testament. There can be little doubt that the theological intentions associated with the redactional perspectives of the wisdom tradition are correctly evaluated by Sheppard. Such an approach has implications not only for our theological understanding of wisdom and its relationship to other traditions, but also for the sociological setting of the Old Testament canon in late post-exilic Israel as well.

There is, however, one danger implicit in this approach which must be avoided. The placement of Psalm 1, or of Qoheleth 12:9-14, must not be viewed solely as a redactional move on the part of the wisdom tradition which "finally" places a tradition under the influence of a canonically correct perspective. Psalm 1 becomes appropriate as the heading for the entire Psalter not simply becuse the wise are now in a position to provide normative redactional direction. Rather, it is the result of a long pluralistic process which has always found the cult and the wise in some theological interrelationship.[17] To view the relationship of wisdom and other non-wisdom traditions only or even primarily from a redactional, "canonical" perspective is to misrepresent and slight the nature and the dynamic movement of this relationship throughout Israelite history.

Childs has aptly warned us that a "historical" approach to the formation of the Old Testament may indeed divert our attention from the final and "normative" perspectives of the canon.[18] Nevertheless, when such a historical development is viewed holistically and placed within a pluralistic matrix which provides a rationale for the development, then it does not seem to be entirely reasonable to regard the final perspectives as the last and best. It would be more realistic to regard the "final" perspectives as a mixture of religious traditions which has been produced by a dynamic process which testifies to the diversity and the cohesiveness of the whole—the canon.[19]

Contemporary Implications

Gerhard von Rad has stated that "the first wisdom teacher to refer to traditions from his nation's history was Sirach."[20] This statement is certainly correct, but some of the implications that might be drawn from it are not. Such a statement is often tied to views such as those of Rylaarsdam who notes a lack of integration of wisdom into the national religion. Commenting upon the development found in Sirach and the Wisdom of Solomon he speaks of the "surrender" of the Jewish wisdom movement to the Law and considers it a "shift from a reliance upon reason to grace."[21] For Rylaarsdam, when the natural-empirical method of wisdom fails, the "only alternative to despair is a transcendent faith."[22] In light of the use of the wisdom's teachings in non-wisdom literature, such statements and positions are very difficult to accept. Even though the wisdom literature itself does not explicitly incorporate nationalistic traditions until Sirach, the wisdom tradition, directly and indirectly, was involved and concerned with those traditions which set forth nationalistic and revelatory conceptions of Yahweh. It was, moreover, tied closely to the institutions responsible for their literary creation and transmission of these other traditions. Therefore, instead of assuming that wisdom is separate from other traditions, perhaps under an indirect influence of the twentieth century debate over "natural" versus "revealed" religion,[23] we must instead look to historical and sociological developments which create the setting for Sirach. In doing this we recognize that the theological developments manifest in his teachings about law and Israelite salvation history have important and necessary antecedents.

These observations about the nature and development of the wisdom tradition and its interrelationship with all parts of Israelite religion throughout the Old Testament period have important implications for future study of the Bible and its use in contemporary theology. Our attention has been and must continue to be focused on the wisdom tradition itself, for the contributions of scholarship cited in this study reflect a very important role for this tradition. Its precise theological character is still best determined and evaluated by an initial study of wisdom literature itself, though, as we have seen, its development cannot be separated from the non-wisdom traditions in which it is also found. The most important implications of this particular study for our future use of the study of the wisdom tradition have to do with the viewing of wisdom as part of a whole, as part of a pluralistic religious development in ancient Israel. Future theologies of the Old Testament must integrate the forms and message of the wisdom tradition more completely into monarchical, prophetic, Deuteronomic, and other traditions if an adequate picture of the Old Testament is to be obtained. This would certainly mean that the ideological differentiation often made between "wisdom and _____" could no longer be made on the basis of differing concepts of authority[24] and the polarities such as reason-revelation which are usually behind such differentiation.

It might also be hoped that future systematic theologies would profit from such a view of biblical religion. Surely there are different ways of doing theology, different epistemological bases of authority, different perspectives of the community's relationship to the world. More than this, each age seems to find certain perspectives and traditions from the past which it feels best reflect what God is doing now. We must be careful, however, not to separate these particular, currently popular traditions from those which are more difficult to accept or utilize. This is the real message of the biblical tradition as a whole. Too much focus on human wisdom in the monarchy prompts a prophetic critique, while at the same time a Deuteronomic movement utilizes the wisdom tradition to provide a new framework for understanding torah, God's will for the community. Never, then, can we find the focus on the prophets, or wisdom, or the cult, or any other interpretive tradition so strong that other traditions cannot be heard. Sociological and institutional rigidity sometimes occur, but ideological pluralism will nonetheless continue. This is a message by which all attempts at doing contemporary theology need to be informed.

Finally, there are important implications for the church, or any community grounded in the biblical traditions, which flow from this study. Members of these contemporary communities are the heirs of biblical pluralism. The relationship of the wisdom tradition to other major traditions reflects a community open to a multiplicity of theological perspectives. Such a multiplicity surely exists in the church today, but we often attempt to deal with it by taking sides, by labeling perspectives different from ours as heretical or at best non-edifying. Such attempts fail to take seriously the common matrix within which we all belong, which accepts diversity and conflict but also demands that we seek to learn from and integrate differing perspectives and traditions into our own. To a certain extent the biblical message viewed as a whole affirms that these "other" traditions are ours also.

Too often wisdom has been labeled as "secular" and viewed as a minority opinion, its popularity and validity appropriate simply as a corrective to neo-orthodoxy. Instead, the integration of wisdom into non-wisdom literature witnesses to important dimensions for all biblical tradition, in ancient Israel or the twentieth century. On the one hand, Israelite religion and society never allowed itself to think solely in terms of the "sacred," to attempt to perceive God purely within the bounds of the nationalistic community. Rather Israel was constantly challenged to relate the concepts of chosenness, of a special sacred history, to the entire created order. On the other hand, the wisdom tradition, though never in the seat of absolute authority, often sought to legitimize itself and the locus of power to which it was attached. Such attempts continually related the order of the society to larger conceptions of God's wisdom and power, obliterating in many ways the distinction between sacred and profane which present-day communities often use to define and justify their own institutional orders.

Ultimately the wisdom tradition cannot be seen as more authoritative than other traditions in the Old Testament. It does not witness to a clear-minded group who uniquely perceived what God was really about. In light of its presence in non-wisdom literature and its complicated interrelationship with the major forces and traditions of Israelite religion, wisdom reflects a dimension of our faith which cannot be forgotten. It provides a model for the doing of theology which demands that we take seriously the multifaceted nature of our biblical heritage.

ABBREVIATIONS

AB	Anchor Bible
AcOr	*Acta Orientalia*
ASTI	*Annual of the Swedish Theological Institute*
BS	Biblische Studien
BZAW	Beihefte zur Seitschrift für die alttestamentliche Wissenschaft
CBQ	*Catholic Biblical Quarterly*
CBQMS	Catholic Biblical Quarterly Monograph Series
EvTh	*Evangelische Theologie*
ET	*Expository Times*
HUCA	*Hebrew Union College Annual*
HTR	*Harvard Theological Review*
ICC	International Critical Commentary
Interp.	*Interpretation*
JBL	*Journal of Biblical Literature*
JSOT	*Journal for the Study of the Old Testament*
JSS	*Journal of Semitic Studies*
RB	*Revue Biblique*
RSR	*Religious Studies Review*
SANT	Studien zum Alten und Neuen Testament
SBT	Studies in Biblical Theology
ScE	*Sciences ecclésiastiques*
SJT	*Scottish Journal of Theology*
SOTSMS	Society of Old Testament Studies Monograph Series
TS	Theologische Studien
TUMSR	Trinity University Monograph Series in Religion
VuF	*Verkündigung und Forschung*
VT	*Vetus Testamentum*
VTS	Supplement to *Vetus Testamentum*
WMANT	Wissenschaftliche Monographien zum Alten und Neuen Testament
ZAW	*Zeitschrift für die alttestamentliche Wissenschaft*

NOTES

Chapter I

1. For an overview of the results and implications of this research see J. Crenshaw, "Prolegomenon," in *Studies in Ancient Israelite Wisdom,* ed. J. Crenshaw (New York, 1976), pp. 1-60.
2. Cf. Walter Bauer, *Orthodoxy and Heresy in Earliest Christianity,* ed. R. Kraft and G. Krodel (Philadelphia, 1971). For a recent evaluation of Old Testament traditions from a pluralistic perspective see Paul Hanson, *Dynamic Transcendence* (Philadelphia, 1978).
3. Crenshaw, "Prologomenon," in *Studies in Ancient Israelite Wisdom,* p. 9.
4. For bibliography see Crenshaw, *Studies in Ancient Israelite Wisdom,* pp. 9-13; R. N. Whybray, *The Intellectual Tradition in the Old Testament* (Berlin, 1974), pp. 1-2, n. 1; and the research discussed in the present study.
5. Cf., e.g., J. Crenshaw, "Method in Determining Wisdom Influence upon 'Historical' Literature," *JBL,* LXXXVIII (1969), 129-142; and Whybray, *Intellectual Tradition.*
6. Cf. H. H. Schmid, *Wesen und Geschichte der Weisheit* (Berlin, 1966), p. 149.
7. William McKane, *Prophets and Wise Men* (London, 1965). This study, as so many before and after it, operates out of an understanding which distinguishes wisdom from other Old Testament traditions on the basis of a reason-revelation dichotomy.
8. This, perhaps, is the most serious and fundamental difference between the present study and the positions of Crenshaw and others, in practice if not in theory.
9. R. Murphy, "Wisdom—Theses and Hypotheses," in *Israelite Wisdom,* ed. J. G. Gammie, et al., p. 39.
10. W. Brueggemann, "The Epistemological Crisis of Israel's Two Histories (Jer. 9:22-23)," in *Israelite Wisdom,* p. 100.
11. J. Ward, "The Servant's Knowledge in Isaiah 40–50," in *Israelite Wisdom,* p. 122.
12. Gerhard von Rad, *Wisdom in Israel* (Philadelphia, 1972), p. 291.
13. Whybray, *Intellectual Tradition,* pp. 69f.

14. E. H. Heaton, *Solomon's New Men* (London, 1974), p. 130.
15. J. F. Priest, "Where Is Wisdom to Be Placed?" *JBR,* XXXI (1963), 281.

Chapter II

1. Cf., e.g., R. Murphy, "Assumptions and Problems in Old Testament Wisdom Research," *CBQ,* XXIX (1967), 407-410.
2. Cf., e.g., R. B. Y. Scott, "Folk Proverbs of the Ancient Near East," in *Studies in Ancient Israelite Wisdom,* pp. 417-426.
3. See especially J. P. Audet, "Origines comparées de la double tradition de la loi et de la sagesse dans la proche-orient ancien," Acten Internationalen Orientalistenkongresses (Moscow, 1960), 1, 352-357; and E. Gerstenberger, *Wesen und Herkunft des "apodiktischen Rechts."*
4. O. Eissfeldt, *Der Maschal im Alten Testament* (Giessen, 1913). See also, J. L. Crenshaw, "Wisdom," in *Old Testament Form Criticism,* ed. J. H. Hayes (San Antonio, 1974), pp. 229-239, for an overview of research on this form.
5. R. Murphy, "Form Criticism and Wisdom Literature," *CBQ,* XXXI (1969), 477-483; H. J. Hermission, *Studien zur israelitischen Spruchweisheit* (Neukirchen-Vluyn, 1966), pp. 38-52.
6. R. B. Y. Scott, "The Study of the Wisdom Literature," *Interp.,* XXXIV (1970), 29, 33; Crenshaw, "Prolegomenon," in *Studies in Ancient Israelite Wisdom,* pp. 13-22.
7. For a brief discussion of the function of the proverbial form see Crenshaw, "Wisdom," pp. 229-239; and von Rad, *Wisdom,* pp. 25-34.
8. J. L. Crenshaw has recently suggested that there are potentially *three* riddles in the Samson story. In addition to the riddle of Samson, the responses of the Philistines ("What is sweeter than honey? What is stronger than a lion?") and Samson ("If you had not plowed with my heifer, you would not have found out my riddle") in Judges 14:18 are both asserted to have latent riddle forms within them (*Samson* [Atlanta, 1978], pp. 111-120).
9. This is Crenshaw's translation (ibid. p. 112).
10. See R. J. Williams, "The Fable in the Ancient Near East," in *A Stubborn Faith,* ed. Edward C. Hobbs (Dallas, 1956), p. 11.
11. R. G. Boling, *Judges,* Anchor Bible, 6A (Garden City, 1975), p. 174.
12. Barnabus Lindars, "Jotham's Fable—A New Form-Critical Analysis," *JTS,* XXIV (1973), 355-366.
13. Cf., e.g., G. P. Couturier, "Sagesse babylonienne et sagesse israelite," *ScE,* XIV (1962), 308-309.

14. Cf., e.g., The works of Audet and Gerstenberger in n. 3; and W. Richter, *Recht und Ethos* (München, 1966).
15. Audet, "Origines comparées," and B. Gemser, "Motive Clauses in Old Testament Law," VTS, I (1953), 50-66.
16. Gemser, VTS, I, 64-66.
17. See the recent and monumental study of N. Gottwald for a full discussion of the sociological matrix of pre-monarchical Israel (*The Tribes of Yahweh* [New York, 1979]). Especially pertinent to our study is the treatment of law (pp. 93 ff.) and social structures (pp. 237-43).
18. For an important critique of Gerstenberger's position see Whybray, *Intellectual Tradition*, pp. 113 ff.
19. Richter, *Recht und Ethos*, pp. 147 ff.

Chapter III

1. Luis Alonso-Schökel, "Sapiential and Covenant Themes in Genesis 2–3" in *Studies in Ancient Israelite Wisdom*, pp. 468-480.
2. See also W. Brueggemann, *In Man We Trust* (Richmond, 1972), pp. 54 f.
3. Ibid., pp. 56-60; Whybray, *Intellectual Tradition*, pp. 105-108.
4. For example, the notion of retribution. See Alonso-Schökel, "Sapiential and Covenant Themes"; and Crenshaw, "Prolegomenon," in *Studies in Ancient Israelite Wisdom*, pp. 12 f., 26. The latter notes similarities and provides an alternative explanation of how wisdom dealt with the problem of divine justice.
5. G. Mendenhall, "The Shady Side of Wisdom: The Date and Purpose of Genesis 3," in *A Light Unto My Path: Old Testament Studies in Honor of Jacob M. Myers* (Philadelphia, 1974), pp. 319-334.
6. E.g., J. van Seters, *Abraham in History and Tradition* (New Haven, 1975).
7. See von Rad, *Wisdom*, pp. 291 f. and also his essay "The Theological Problem of the Old Testament Doctrine of Creation," in *The Problem of the Hexateuch and Other Essays* (New York, 1966), pp. 131-143.
8. C. Westermann, *Creation* (Philadelphia, 1974); also Brevard Childs, *Introduction to the Old Testament as Scripture* (Philadelphia, 1979), p. 155.
9. See n. 3 above.
10. B. S. Childs, "The Birth of Moses," *JBL*, LXXXIV (1965), 109-122.
11. G. von Rad, "The Joseph Narrative and Ancient Wisdom," in *Studies in Ancient Israelite Wisdom*, pp. 439-447.

12. See D. B. Redford, *A Study of the Biblical Story of Joseph*, VTS, XX; and G. W. Coats, "The Joseph Story and Ancient Wisdom: A Reappraisal," *CBQ*, XXV (1973), 285-297; and *From Canaan to Egypt*, CBQMS (Washington, 1976).
13. Coats, "The Joseph Story"; R. N. Whybray, "The Joseph Story and Pentateuchal Criticism," *VT*, XVII (1968), 522-528.
14. Whybray, *Intellectual Tradition*, p. 87.
15. Cf., however, Brueggemann, *In Man We Trust*, pp. 29ff.; and J. Blenkinsopp, "Jonathan's Sacrilege," *CBQ*, XXVI (1964), 423-449.
16. *The Succession Narrative* (London, 1968). For criticism of this position, as well as other perspectives, see E. Wurthwein, *Die Erzählung von der Thronfolge Davids—theologische oder politische Geschichtsschreibung?*, TS, 115 (Zurich, 1974); T. Veijola, *Die Ewige Dynastie* (Helsinki, 1975); A. M. Gunn, "The Story of King David," *JSOT* Supplement Series, 6 (Sheffield, 1978).
17. Whybray, *Succession Narrative*, p. 72.
18. Whybray, *Intellectual Tradition*, especially pp. 89-91.
19. *In Man We Trust*, pp. 29ff. On the issue of a "Solomonic Enlightenment" see J. Crenshaw's review of G. von Rad's *Wisdom in Israel* in *RSR*, II (1976), 6-12.
20. Whybray, *Intellectual Tradition*, pp. 91-93; A. Alt, "Solomonic Wisdom," in *Studies in Ancient Israelite Wisdom*, pp. 102-112; R. B. Y. Scott, "Solomon and the Beginnings of Wisdom in Israel," in *Studies in Ancient Israelite Wisdom*, pp. 84-101; et al.
21. See especially J. R. Boston, "The Wisdom Influence Upon the Song of Moses," *JBL*, LXXXVII (1968), 198-202; and Whybray, *Intellectual Tradition*, pp. 88-89.
22. See von Rad, *Wisdom*, p. 295, n. 9, where he suggests that a prophetic reinterpretation of wisdom is reflected in this passage. For further discussion of this prophetic activity see Chapter IV.
23. Whybray, *Intellectual Tradition*, pp. 113f.
24. Cf. W. Brueggemann, *In Man We Trust*, pp. 69f.
25. Cf. Richter, *Recht und Ethos;* and Hermisson, *Studien zur Israelitischen Spruchweisheit*, pp. 97ff.
26. Cf. Crenshaw, "Prolegomenon," in *Studies in Ancient Israelite Wisdom*, pp. 6ff. and the bibliography cited there.
27. Cf. note 19 above.
28. B. Kovacs, "Is There a Class Ethic in Proverbs?" in *Essays in Old Testament Ethics*, ed. J. Crenshaw and J. Willis (New York, 1974), pp. 171-189.

29. *Prophets and Wise Men,* pp. 48 ff.
30. C. Bauer-Kayatz, *Studien zu Proverbien 1–9* (Neukirchen-Vluyn, 1966).
31. *Solomon's New Men,* p. 130.
32. R. Murphy, "Wisdom Theses," in *The Papin Festschrift. Wisdom and Knowledge* (Philadelphia, 1976), Vol. II, pp. 190-192.
33. Whybray, *Succession Narrative.*

Chapter IV

1. W. O. E. Oesterley, *Proverbs,* Westminster Commentaries (London, 1929), lix.
2. Cf. R. E. Clements, *Prophecy and Tradition* (Atlanta, 1975), pp. 73-86.
3. Cf., however, J. Fichtner, "Isaiah Among the Wise," in *Studies in Ancient Israelite Wisdom,* ed. J. Crenshaw, pp. 429-438; and R. J. Anderson, "Was Isaiah a Scribe?" *JBL,* LXXIX (1960), 57-58, both of whom claim a very close connection between Isaiah and the wise.
4. For a discussion of the prophetic reinterpretation of wisdom see McKane, *Prophets and Wise Men,* pp. 86 ff.
5. Cf. J. Crenshaw, *Prophetic Conflict* (Berlin, 1971), pp. 116-123.
6. See McKane, *Prophets and Wise Men;* and von Rad, *Wisdom,* pp. 287 ff.
7. W. R. Harper, *Amos and Hosea,* ICC (New York, 1905), cxv.
8. S. Terrien, "Amos and Wisdom," in *Studies in Ancient Israelite Wisdom,* pp. 448-457; H. W. Wolff, *Amos the Prophet.*
9. Terrien, "Amos and Wisdom," p. 449.
10. Cf. also R. H. Pfeiffer, "Edomite Wisdom," *ZAW,* LXIV (1926), 13-25.
11. Cf. Gerstenberger, *Wesen und Herkunft* and "The Woe Oracles of the Prophets," *JBL,* LXXXI (1962), 249-263.
12. Cf. critiques of the "wisdom influence" in Amos by J. Crenshaw, "The Influence of the Wise upon Amos. The 'Doxologies of Amos,' and Job 5:9-16; 9:5-10," *ZAW,* LXXI (1967), 45-52; and Whybray, *Intellectual Tradition,* pp. 117-119.
13. W. M. W. Roth, *Numerical Sayings in the Old Testament,* VTS, XIII.
14. Gerstenberger, *Wesen und Herkunft,* pp. 43-45; Wolff, *Amos the Prophet.*
15. Gerstenberger, "Woe Oracles," 249-263.
16. Cf. W. Janzen, "'Asre in the Old Testament," *HTR,* LVIII (1965), 215-226; and G. Wanke, "אוֹי und הוֹי," *ZAW,* LXXVIII (1966), 215-218.

17. Whybray, *Intellectual Tradition*, pp. 140-142.
18. On the connection of Amos and Isaiah, the latter clearly influenced by monarchical wisdom, see R. Fry, *Amos und Jesaja*, WMANT 12 (Neukirchen-Vluyn, 1963).
19. There can be no question that this final wisdom saying represents a later redactional perspective. Cf. Childs, *Introduction*, pp. 382-383.
20. Cf., e.g., Boston, "The Wisdom Influence Upon the Song of Moses," pp. 198-200; and H. W. Wolff, *Hosea*, Hermeneia (Philadelphia, 1974), p. 97.
21. Cf., however, McKane, *Prophets and Wise Men*, pp. 86ff., who sees 4:6, 14 as examples of a prophetic reinterpretation of wisdom vocabulary.
22. Cf. J. L. McKenzie, "Knowledge of God in Hosea," *JBL*, LXXIV (1955), 22-27.
23. E. W. Heaton, *The Hebrew Kingdoms* (London, 1968), p. 179.
24. Cf. H. W. Wolff, "Micah the Moreshite—The Prophet and His Background," in *Israelite Wisdom*, pp. 77-84; and "Wie verstand Micha von Moroshet sein prophetisches Amt?" VTS XXIX (1978), 403-417.
25. Ilse von Löwenclau, "Zur Auslegung von Jesaja 1, 2-3," *EvTh*, XXVI (1966), 294-308.
26. Cf., e.g., G. E. Wright, "The Lawsuit of God, A Form-Critical Study of Deuteronomy 32," in *Israel's Prophetic Heritage*, ed. B. W. Anderson and W. Harrelson (New York, 1962), pp. 26-67.
27. J. William Whedbee, *Isaiah and Wisdom*, pp. 87ff.
28. See B. S. Childs, *Isaiah and the Assyrian Crisis*, SBT 2nd Series, 3 (London, 1967), pp. 128-136; and Whedbee, *Isaiah and Wisdom*, pp. 75-79. J. Crenshaw (private communication) believes the context in which this form occurs has not been taken seriously and as a result its intention and function are misunderstood.
29. See McKane, *Prophets and Wise Men*, p. 66ff.; Whedbee, *Isaiah and Wisdom*, pp. 111ff.
30. J. Jensen, *The Use of Tôrâ by Isaiah* (Washington, 1973).
31. Ibid., pp. 59ff.
32. See Whybray, *Intellectual Tradition*, pp. 98f., 121ff.
33. "Isaiah Among the Wise," pp. 436ff.
34. Cf., e.g., W. Brueggemann, "Jeremiah's Use of Rhetorical Questions," *JBL*, LCII (1973), 358-374; T. R. Hobbs, "Jeremiah 3:1-5 and Deuteronomy 24:1-4," *ZAW*, LXXXVI (1974), 23-29, and "Some Proverbial Reflections in the Book of Jeremiah," *ZAW*, XCI (1979), 62-72.

35. Cf. Hobbs, "Some Proverbial Reflections," pp. 62-72.
36. Brueggemann, "The Epistemological Crisis of Israel's Two Histories," pp. 85-105; W. Holladay, *The Architecture of Jeremiah 1–20* (Lewisburg, 1976), pp. 85, 93, 110 ff.
37. *Intellectual Tradition,* pp. 21 ff.
38. See J. P. Hyatt, "Torah in the Book of Jeremiah," *JBL,* LX (1941), 381-396.
39. See D. E. Gowan, "Habakkuk and Wisdom," *Perspective,* IX (1968), 157-166; and D. S. Dykes, "Diversity and Unity in Habakkuk," Ph.D. dissertation, Vanderbilt University, 1976.
40. See O. S. Rankin, *Israel's Wisdom Literature* (New York, 1969), pp. 53 ff.

Chapter V

1. Cf., e.g., M. Weinfeld, *Deuteronomy and the Deuteronomic School* (Oxford, 1972); C. Carmichael, *The Laws of Deuteronomy* (Ithaca, 1974).
2. E.g., R. Rendtorff, *Das überlieferungeschichtliche Problem des Pentateuch,* BZAW, 147 (Berlin, 1977); H. H. Schmid, *Der sogenannte Jahwist: Beobachten und Fragen zur Pentateuchforschung* (Zurich, 1976).
3. E.g., E. Kutsch, *Verheissung und Gesetz,* BZAW, 113 (Berlin, 1973); L. Perlitt, *Bundestheologie im Alten Testament,* WMANT, 36 (Neukirchen-Vluyn, 1969).
4. E.g., M. Weinfeld, *Deuteronomy and the Deuteronomic School.*
5. Cf. especially R. B. Y. Scott, "Solomon and the Beginnings of Wisdom in Israel," pp. 84-101.
6. Cf., however, McKane, *Prophets and Wise Men,* for a fairly complete description of the "wise."
7. Cf. E. W. Nicholson, *Deuteronomy and Tradition* (Oxford, 1967); and J. Muilenberg, "Baruch the Scribe," in *Proclamation and Presence: Old Testament Essays in Honor of Gwynn Henton Davies,* ed. J. F. Durham and J. R. Porter (Richmond, 1970), pp. 215-238.
8. Weinfeld, *Deuteronomy and the Deuteronomic School,* p. 160.
9. Cf., however, Whybray's discussion of this passage in *Intellectual Tradition,* pp. 22 ff.
10. For a prophetic origin of this style see P. Ackroyd, "The Vitality of the Word of God in the Old Testament," *ASTI,* I (1962), 7-23. For a cultic origin see G. von Rad, "The Problem of the Hexateuch," in *The Problem of the Hexateuch and Other Essays,* p. 26 f.

11. Cf., e.g., J. W. McKay, "Man's Love for God in Deuteronomy and Father/Teacher—Son/Pupil Relationship," *VT*, XXII (1972), 426-435.
12. Cf., e.g., Weinfeld, *Deuteronomy and the Deuteronomic School*, p. 34 f.
13. Ibid., pp. 171-178; Carmichael, *The Laws of Deuteronomy;* and B. R. Moore, "The Scribal Contributions to Deuteronomy 4:1-40," Ph.D. dissertation, Notre Dame University, 1976, p. 78 f.
14. Cf. the study of J. L'Hour, "Les Interdits to ᶜeba dans le Deuteronome," *RB*, LXXI (1964), 481-503, for additional discussion.
15. See Weinfeld, *Deuteronomy and the Deuteronomic School*, pp. 260-274, for a fuller discussion of these parallels. I am indebted to this work for the parallel textual presentation above.
16. See, e.g., J. Malfroy, "Sagesse et Loi dans le Deuteronome Etudes," *VT*, XV (1965), 49-65; and Whybray, *Intellectual Tradition*, pp. 87 f., 121f.
17. Weinfeld, *Deuteronomy and the Deuteronomic School*, p. 283.
18. B. Lindars, "Torah in Deuteronomy," in *Words and Meanings. Essays Presented to D. Winton Thomas*, ed. P. R. Ackroyd and B. Lindars (Cambridge, 1968), p. 131.
19. Weinfeld, *Deuteronomy and the Deuteronomic School*, p. 151.
20. Ibid., p. 307 f.
21. Ibid., p. 255.

Chapter VI

1. Cf., e.g., P. Ackroyd, *Exile and Restoration* (Philadelphia, 1968); Paul Hanson, *The Dawn of Apocalyptic* (Philadelphia, 1975); T. Raitt, *A Theology of Exile: Judgment or Deliverance in Jeremiah and Ezekiel* (Philadelphia, 1977); M. Klein, *Israel in Exile* (Philadelphia, 1980).
2. Cf., e.g., J. Sanders, *Torah and Canon* (Philadelphia, 1972).
3. For a brief overview of these problems see the critical introductions, most recently Childs, *Introduction*, pp. 353-372.
4. Cf., e.g., G. Landes, "Creation Tradition in Proverbs 8:22-31 and Genesis 1," in *A Light Unto My Path. Old Testament Studies in Honor of Jacob M. Myers*, pp. 279-293.
5. Ibid., p. 289.
6. Brueggemann, *In Man We Trust*, pp. 67, 121.
7. Landes, "Creation Tradition," p. 290; C. Bauer-Kayatz, *Studien zu Proverbien 1-9;* cf. also R. N. Whybray, "Proverbs VIII 22-31 and Its Supposed Prototypes," *VT*, XV (1965), 504-514.

8. Crenshaw, "Prolegomenon," in *Studies in Ancient Israelite Wisdom,* p. 26f.
9. For pertinent bibliography cf. D. Morgan, "Wisdom and the Prophets," in *Studia Biblica 1978,* ed. E. A. Livingstone *JSOT* Supplementary Series, 11, pp. 209-244.
10. R. H. Pfeiffer, "The Dual Origin of Hebrew Monotheism," *JBL,* XLVI (1927), 193-203; S. Terrien,"Quelques Remarques sur les Affinités de Job avec le Deutéro-Esaïe," VTS, XV (1965), 295-310.
11. R. N. Whybray, *The Heavenly Counsellor in Isaiah xl 13-14.*
12. J. M. Ward, "The Servant's Knowledge in Isaiah 40–50," in *Israelite Wisdom,* pp. 121-136.
13. Ibid., p. 134.
14. Cf. the discussion of various traditions and themes in this prophet by W. Brueggemann, "Trajectories in OT Literature and Sociology of Ancient Israel," *JBL,* XCVIII (1979), 178-179.
15. Cf. P. Hanson, *The Dawn of Apocalpytic.*

Chapter VII

1. Cf., e.g., G. Caird, "New Wine in Old Wineskins. I. Wisdom," *ET,* LXXXIV/6 (1973), 164-168.
2. Cf. J. Blenkinsopp, *Prophecy and Canon* (Notre Dame, 1977).
3. Cf., e.g., A. Robert, "Les Attachés Litteraires Bibliques de Prov. I–IX," *RB,* XLIII (1934), 42-68, 172-204, 374-84; XLIV (1935), 344-365, 502-25.
4. Cf. P. Hanson, *The Dawn of Apocalyptic.*
5. See B. R. Moore, "The Scribal Contribution to Deuteronomy 4:1-40," pp. 43ff.
6. Cf. H. E. von Waldow, "The Message of Deutero-Isaiah," *Interp.,* XXII (1968), 269, n. 33; and Crenshaw, "Prolegomenon," in *Studies in Ancient Israelite Wisdom,* pp. 31ff.
7. See E. Haller, *Die Erzählung von dem Propheten Jona,* Theologische Existenz Heute, LXV (München, 1958). For a recent assessment of this book from a wisdom perspective see George M. Landes, "Jonah: A Mašal?" in *Israelite Wisdom,* ed. Gammie, et al., pp. 137-158.
8. Cf. R. Dentan, "The Literary Affinities of Exodus XXXIV 6f.," *VT,* XIII (1963), 34-51.
9. Phyllis Trible, "Studies in the Book of Jonah," Ph.D. dissertation, Columbia University, 1963.

10. S. Talmon, "Wisdom in the Book of Esther," *VT,* XIII (1963), 419-455.
11. Ibid., pp. 442, 427.
12. Cf. L. Perdue, *Wisdom and Cult,* SBL Dissertation Series, 30 (Missoula, 1977), pp. 261ff.
13. Ibid.
14. For a discussion of this canonical significance see Childs, *Introduction,* pp. 513-514.
15. Perdue, *Wisdom and Cult,* pp. 360ff.
16. S. Mowinckel, "Traditionalism and Personality in the Psalms," *HUCA,* XXIII (1950-51), 205-231.
17. Crenshaw, "Prolegomenon," in *Studies in Ancient Israelite Wisdom,* pp. 26ff.; cf. also H.-J. Hermisson, *Sprache und Ritus im Altisraeliti-schen Kult,* WMANT, 19, (Neukirchen-Vluyn, 1965), especially pp. 145-147.
18. E. Gerstenberger, "Psalms," in *Old Testament Form Criticism,* ed. J. H. Hayes, p. 219.
19. Cf. J. Jensen, *The Use of Tôrâ by Isaiah,* pp. 122ff.
20. Cf. von Rad, *Wisdom,* pp. 263-283; Whybray, *Intellectual Tradition,* pp. 101ff.
21. von Rad, *Wisdom,* pp. 263ff.
22. P. Hanson, *The Dawn of Apocalyptic.*
23. von Rad, *Wisdom,* p. 277.
24. Cf. R. Gordis, "The Social Background of Wisdom Literature," *HUCA,* XVIII (1943/44), 77-118.

Chapter VIII

1. Cf. B. Gemser, "Motive Clauses in Old Testament Law," VTS I (1953), 50-66.
2. Cf. McKane, *Prophets and Wise Men.*
3. Cf. Perdue, *Wisdom and Cult,* pp. 229-230, n. 29.
4. von Rad, *Wisdom,* p. 291.
5. Cf. J. Priest, "Humanism, Scepticism, and Pessimism in Israel," *JAAR,* XXXIV (1968), 311-326.
6. Cf. also R. Gordis, "The Social Background of Wisdom Literature."
7. Cf., e.g., Whedbee, *Isaiah and Wisdom,* and Jensen, *The Use of Tôrâ by Isaiah.*
8. Cf., e.g., McKane, *Prophets and Wise Men; M. Fox, "Aspects of the Religion of the Book of Proverbs,"* HUCA, XXXIX (1968), 55-70.

9. Cf. von Rad, *Wisdom*.
10. R. B. Y. Scott, "The Study of Wisdom Literature," *Interp.*, XXIV (1970), 29.
11. Whybray, *Intellectual Tradition*, pp. 6-70.
12. Crenshaw, "Prolegomenon," in *Studies in Israelite Wisdom*, p. 24.
13. Cf. Hanson, *The Dawn of Apocalyptic*, and *Dynamic Transcendence;* Bauer, *Orthodoxy and Heresy in Earliest Christianity*.
14. The necessity of providing a model which allows the possibility of continual interrelationship between traditions is not found in Hanso's *Dynamic Transcendence* or in the recent trajectory approach of W. Brueggemann ("Trajectories in OT Literature and the Sociology of Ancient Israel"). Surely interrelationship is presumed in these theories, but the conceptual models suggested appear too rigid to provide for it.
15. G. Sheppard, "The Epilogue to Qoheleth as Theological Commentary," *CBQ*, XXXIX (1977), 188; more recently, *Wisdom as a Hermeneutical Construct*, BZAW, 151 (New York, 1980), pp. 120-129.
16. Ibid., p. 189.
17. Perdue, *Wisdom and Cult*.
18. Cf. especially Childs, *Introduction*.
19. Cf. Sanders, *Torah and Canon*.
20. von Rad, *Wisdom*, p. 270.
21. J. C. Rylaarsdam, *Revelation in Jewish Wisdom Literature*, p. 31.
22. Ibid., pp. 74-75.
23. Ibid., *vi*f.
24. Crenshaw, *Prophetic Conflict*, pp. 116-123.

SELECT BIBLIOGRAPHY

Wisdom: General Studies

Altbrecht, Alt. "Solomonic Wisdom." In *Studies in Ancient Israelite Wisdom*, edited by J. Crenshaw, pp. 102-112. New York, 1976.

Baumgartner, Walter. "The Wisdom Literature." In *The Old Testament and Modern Study*, edited by H. H. Rowley, pp. 210-237. Oxford, 1951.

Bauer-Kayatz, C. *Einfuhrung in die alttestamentliche Weisheit.* BS, 55. Neukirchen-Vluyn, 1969.

———. *Studien zu Proverbien 1-9.* WMANT, 22. Neukirchen-Vluyn, 1966.

Crenshaw, James L. "Method in Determining Wisdom Influence upon 'Historical' Writing." *JBL*, LXXXVIII (1969), 129-142.

———. "Wisdom." In *Old Testament Form Criticism*, edited by J. L. Hayes. TUMSR, 2 (1974), 225-264.

———, ed. *Studies in Ancient Israelite Wisdom.* The Library of Biblical Studies, edited by Harry M. Orlinksy. New York, 1976.

Brueggemann, Walter. "Scripture and an Ecumenical Life-Style." *Interp.*, XXIV (1970), 3-19.

———. *In Man We Trust.* Richmond, 1972.

Dubarle, A. M. *Les Sages d'Israel.* Paris, 1946.

Duesberg, Hilaire. "L'histoire, Maitresse sagesse?" *Bibel et Vie Chretienne*, LVIII (July-August, 1964), 42-52.

——— and Fransen I. *Les Scribes inspirées: Introduction aux livres sapientaux de la Bible: Job, l'Ecclesiaste, l'Ecclesiatique—la sagesse.* 2nd edition. Paris, 1966.

Fichtner, J. "Zum Problem Glaube und Geschichte in der israelitisch-jüdischen Weisheitliterature." In *Gottes Weisheit*, pp. 9-17. Stuttgart, 1965.

Fox, Michael V. "Aspects of the Religion of the Book of Proverbs," *HUCA*, XXXIX (1968), 55-70.

Gammie, John G., Brueggemann, Walter A., Humphreys, W. Lee, and Ward, James M., eds. *Israelite Wisdom. Theological and Literary Essays in Honor of Samuel Terrien.* Missoula, 1978.

Gemser, Berend. "The Spiritual Structure of Biblical Aphoristic Wisdom." In *Adhuc Loquitur*, ed. A. van Selms and A. S. van der Woude, pp. 138-149. Leiden, 1968.

Gerstenberger, Erhard. "Zur alttestamentlichen Weisheit." *VuF,* XIV (1969), 28-44.

Gordis, Robert. "The Social Background of Wisdom Literature." *HUCA,* LVIII (1943/44), 77-118.

Hermisson, Hans-Jurgen. *Studien zur israelitischen Spruchweisheit.* WMANT, 28. Neukirchen-Vluyn, 1966.

———. "Weisheit und Geschichte." In *Probleme biblischer Theologie,* edited by H. W. Wolff, pp. 136-154. München, 1971.

Hill, R. C. "The Dimensions of Salvation History in the Wisdom Books." *Scripture,* XIX (1967), 97-106.

Hubbard, D. A. "The Wisdom Movement and Israel's Covenant Faith." *Tyndale Bulletin,* XVII (1966), 3-33.

Imschoot, P. van. "Sagesse et esprit dans l'ancien Testament." *RB,* XLVII (1938), 23-49.

Kovacs, Brian W. "Is There a Class Ethic in Proverbs?" In *Essays in Old Testament Ethics,* edited by J. Crenshaw and J. Willis, pp. 171-189. New York, 1974.

Lambert, W. G. *Babylonian Wisdom Literature.* Oxford, 1960.

Leclant, J., et al. *Les Sagesses du Proche-Orient ancien.* Paris, 1963.

McKane, William. *Proverbs.* The Old Testament Library. Philadephia, 1970.

McKenzie, J. L. "Reflections on Wisdom." *JBL,* LXXXVI (1967), 1-9.

Murphy, Roland. "Assumptions and Problems in Old Testament Wisdom Research." *CBQ,* XXIX (1967), 101-112.

———. "The Interpretation of Old Testament Wisdom Literature." *Interp.,* XXIII (1969), 289-301.

———. "Form Criticism and Wisdom Literature." *CBQ,* XXXI (1969), 475-483.

———. "Wisdom and Yahwism." In *No Famine in the Land,* edited by J. Flanagan and A. Robinson, pp. 117-126. Missoula, 1975.

———. "Wisdom Theses." In *The Papin Festschrift, Wisdom and Knowledge,* edited by J. Armenti, pp. 187-200. Vol. II. Philadephia, 1976.

———. "Wisdom—Theses and Hypotheses." In *Israelite Wisdom,* edited by J. G. Gammie, et al., pp. 35-42. Missoula, 1978.

Noth, Martin and Thomas, D. Winton, eds. *Wisdom in Israel and in the Ancient Near East.* VTS, III, 1960.

Pfeiffer, Robert H. "Wisdom and Vision in the Old Testament." *ZAW,* LII (1934), 93-101.

Priest, J. F. "Where Is Wisdom to Be Placed?" *JBR,* XXXI (1963), 275-282.

———. "Humanism, Skepticism, and Pessimism in Israel." *JAAR,* XXXIV (1968), 311-326.

Rad, Gerhard von. *Wisdom in Israel.* Philadelphia, 1972.

Rankin, O. S. *Israel's Wisdom Literature: Its Bearing on Theology and the History of Religion.* Edinburgh, 1936.

Rylaarsdam, J. C. *Revelation in Jewish Wisdom Literature.* Chicago, 1946.

Schmidt, H. H. *Wesen und Geschichte der Weisheit.* BZAW, 101. Berlin, 1966.

Scott, R. B. Y. "Priesthood, Prophecy, Wisdom and the Knowledge of God." *JBL,* LXXX (1961), 1-15.

———. "The Study of the Wisdom Literature." *Interp.* XXIV (1970), 20-45.

———. *The Way of Wisdom.* New York, 1971.

———. "Wise and Foolish, Righteous and Wicked." VTS, XXIII (1972), 146-66.

Urbach, E. E. *The Sages: Their Concepts and Beliefs.* 2 vols. Jerusalem, 1975.

Whybray, R. N. *Wisdom in Proverbs.* SBT, 45. London, 1965.

Zimmerli, W. "The Place and Limit of the Wisdom in the Framework of the Old Testament Theology." *SJT,* XVII (1964), 146-158.

———. "Concerning the Structure of Old Testament Wisdom." In *Studies in Ancient Israelite Wisdom,* edited by J. Crenshaw, pp. 175-207. New York, 1976.

Wisdom in the Pre-monarchical Period

Audet, J. P. "Origines comparées de la double tradition de la loi et de la sagesse dans la proche-orient ancient." Acten Internationalen Orientalisten-Kongresses, 1, pp. 352-357. Moscow, 1962.

Crenshaw, James L. *Samson.* Atlanta, 1978.

Eissfeldt, Otto. *Der Maschal im Alten Testament.* BZAW, 24. Giessen, 1913.

Gemser, B. "Motive Clauses in Old Testament Law." VTS, I (1953), 50-66.

Gerstenberger, E. *Wesen und Herkunft des 'apodiktischen Rechts.'* WMANT, 20 Neukirchen-Vluyn, 1965.

Richter, Wolfgang. *Recht und Ethos.* SANT, 15. München, 1966.

Scott, R. B. Y. "Folk Proverbs of the Ancient Near East." *Transactions of the Royal Society of Canada,* XV (1961), 47-56.

Wisdom in the Early Monarchy

Alonso-Schökel, L. "Sapiential and Covenant Themes in Genesis 2-3." *Biblica,* XLIII (1962), 295-316.

Blenkinsopp. J. "Theme and Motif in the Succession History (2 Sam 11:2ff.) and the Yahwist Corpus." VTS, XV (1965), 44-57.

Boston, J. R. "The Wisdom Influence upon the Song of Moses." JBL, LXXXVII (1968), 198-202.

Childs, B. S. "The Birth of Moses." JBL, LXXXIV (1965), 109-122.

Coats, G. W. "The Joseph Story and Ancient Wisdom: A Reappraisal." CBQ, XXXV (1973), 285-297.

Dentan, Robert. "The Literary Affinities of Exodus XXXIV 6f." VT, XIII (1963), 34-51.

McKane, William. Prophets and Wise Men. SBT, 44. London, 1965.

Mendenhall, George. "The Shady Side of Wisdom: The Date and Purpose of Genesis 3." In A Light Unto My Path: Old Testament Studies in Honor of Jacob M. Myers, edited by H. N. Bream, et al., pp. 319-334. Philadelphia, 1974.

Rad, Gerhard von. "The Theological Problems of the Old Testament Doctrine of Creation." In The Problem of the Hexateuch and Other Essays, pp. 131-143. New York, 1956.

———. "The Joseph Narrative and Ancient Wisdom." In The Problem of the Hexateuch and Other Essays, pp. 292-300. New York, 1966.

Redford, D. B. A Study of the Biblical Story of Joseph (Genesis 37–50). VTS, XX, 1970.

Whybray, R. N. "The Joseph Story and Pentateuchal Criticism." VT, XVIII (1968), 522-528.

———. The Succession Narrative, SBT, 2nd series, 9. London, 1968.

Wisdom and the Prophets

Crenshaw, James L. Prophetic Conflict. BZAW, 124. Berlin, 1971.

Gerstenberger, E. "The Woe Oracles of the Prophets." JBL, LXXXI (1962), 249-263.

Lindblom, J. "Wisdom in the Old Testament Prophets." VTS, III (1960), 192-204.

Morgan, Donn F. "Wisdom and the Prophets." In Studia Biblia 1978, edited by E. A. Livingstone, pp. 209-244. JSOT Supplementary Series, 11. Sheffield, 1979.

Schmid, H. "Hauptproblem der neueren Prophetenforschung." Schweizerische Theologische Umschau, XXXV (1965), 135-143.

Amos

Crenshaw, James L. "The Influence of the Wise upon Amos. The 'Doxologies of Amos,' and Job 5:9-16; 9:5-10." ZAW, LXXIX (1967), 42-52.

Schmid, H. H. "Amos. Zur Frage nach der 'geistige Heimat' des Propheten." *Wort und Dienst,* N. F. X. (1969), 85-103.

Terrien, Samuel. "Amos and Wisdom." In *Israel's Prophetic Heritage,* edited by B. W. Anderson and W. Harrelson, pp. 108-115. New York, 1962.

Wanke, G. "אוֹי und הוֹי," *ZAW,* LXXVIII (1966), 215-218.

Wolff, H. W. *Amos and the Prophet.* Philadelphia, 1973.

Isaiah

Anderson, R. J. "Was Isaiah a Scribe?" *JBL,* LXXIX (1960), 57-58.

Fichtner, J. "Jahwes Plan in der Botschaft des Jesaja." In *Gottes Weisheit,* pp. 27-43. Stuttgart, 1965.

————. "Isaiah Among the Wise." In *Studies in Ancient Israelite Wisdom,* edited by J. L. Crenshaw, pp. 429-438. New York, 1976.

Jensen, Joseph. *The Use of Tôrâ by Isaiah.* CBQMS, 3. Washington, 1973.

Lowenclau, Ilse von. "Zur Auslegung von Jesaja 1, 2-3." *EvTh,* XXVI (1966), 294-308.

Whedbee, J. William. *Isaiah and Wisdom.* New York, 1971.

Other Prophets

Brueggemann, Walter. "Jeremiah's Use of Rhetorical Questions." *JBL,* XCII (1973), 358-374.

————. "The Epistemological Crisis of Israel's Two Histories (Jer. 9:22-23)." In *Israelite Wisdom,* edited by J. G. Gammie, et al., pp. 85-105. Missoula, 1978.

Gowan, Donald E. "Habakkuk and Wisdom." *Perspective,* IX (1968), 157-166.

Hobbs, T. R. "Jeremiah 3:1-5 and Deuteronomy 24:1-4." *ZAW,* LXXXVI (1974), 23-29.

————. "Some Proverbial Reflections in the Book of Jeremiah." *ZAW,* XCI (1979), 62-72.

McKane, William. "Jeremiah 13:12-14: A Problematic Proverb." In *Israelite Wisdom,* edited by J. G. Gammie, et al., pp. 107-120. Missoula, 1978.

McKenzie, J. L. "Knowledge of God in Hosea." *JBL,* LXXIV (1955), 22-27.

Pfeiffer, E. "Die Disputationsworte im Buche Maleachi." *EvTh,* XIX (1959), 546-568.

Trible, P. L. "Studies in the Book of Jonah." Ph.D. dissertation, Columbia University, 1964.

Wolff, H. W. "Wie verstand Micha von Moreschet sein prophetisches Amt?" In *Congress Volume. Göttingen, 1977,* pp. 403-417. VTS, XXIX, 1978.

————. "Micah the Moreshite—The Prophet and His Background." In *Israelite Wisdom,* edited by J. G. Gammie, et al., pp. 77-84. Missoula, 1978.

Wisdom and the Deuteronomic Movement

Carmichael, Calum M. "Deuteronomic Laws, Wisdom, and Historical Traditions. *JSS,* XII (1967), 198-206.

————. *The Laws of Deuteronomy.* Ithaca, 1974.

Lindars, B. "Torah in Deuteronomy." In *Words and Meanings. Essays Presented to D. Winton Thomas,* edited by P. R. Ackroyd and B. Lindars, pp. 117-136. Cambridge, 1968.

Malfroy, Jean. "Sagesse et Loi dans le Deuteronome Études." *VT,* XV (1965), 49-65.

McKay, J. W. "Man's Love for God in Deuteronomy and Father/Teacher—Son/Pupil Relationship." *VT,* XXII (1972), 426-435.

Moore, Brian R. "The Scribal Contribution to Deuteronomy 4: 1-40." Ph.D. dissertation. Notre Dame University, 1976.

Weinfeld, Moshe. "The Source of the Idea of Reward in Deuteronomy." *Tarbiz,* XXIX (1960), 8-15.

————. "The Origins of Humanism in Deuteronomy." *JBL,* LXXX (1961), 241-247.

————. "Deuteronomy—The Present State of Enquiry." *JBL,* LXXXVI (1967), 249-262.

————. *Deuteronomy and the Deuteronomic School.* Oxford, 1972.

Wisdom in the Exile

Landes, George. "Creation Tradition in Proverbs 8:22-31 and Genesis 1." In *A Light Unto My Path: Old Testament Studies in Honor of Jacob M. Myers,* pp. 279-293. Philadelphia, 1974.

Pfeiffer, R. H. "The Dual Origin of Hebrew Monotheism." *JBL,* XLVI (1927), 193-203.

Terrien, S. "Quelques Remarques sur les Affinités de Job avec le Deutero-Esaïe." *VTS,* XV (1965), 295-310.

Ward, James J. "The Servant's Knowledge in Isaiah 40-50." In *Israelite Wisdom,* edited by J. G. Gammie, et al., pp. 121-136. Missoula, 1978.

Whybray, R. N. *The Heavenly Counsellor in Isaiah xl 13–14.* SOTSMS. Cambridge, 1971.

Wisdom in the Post-exilic Period

De Vries, Simon J. "Observations on Quantitative and Qualitative Time in

Wisdom and Apocalyptic." In *Israelite Wisdom,* edited by J. G. Gammie, et al., pp. 263-276.

Gammie, John G. "Spatial and Ethical Dualism in Jewish Wisdom and Apocalyptic Literature." *JBL,* XCIII (1974), 356-385.

Kuntz, J. Kenneth. "The Canonical Wisdom Psalms of Ancient Israel—Their Rhetorical, Thematic, and Formal Dimensions." In *Rhetorical Criticism,* edited by J. L. Jackson and M. Kessler, pp. 186-222. Pittsburgh, 1974.

Landes, George M. "Jonah; A *Mašal?*" In *Israelite Wisdom,* edited by J. G. Gammie, et al., pp. 137-158. Missoula, 1978.

Mack, B. "Wisdom Myth and Mythology." *Interp.,* XXIV (1970), 46-60.

Mowinckel, S. "Traditionalism and Personality in the Psalms." *HUCA,* XXIII (1951), 205-231.

———. "Psalms and Wisdom." VTS, III (1960), 205-224.

Munch, P. A. "Die judischen 'Weisheitspsalmen' und ihr Platz im Leben," *AcOr,* XV (1937), 112-140.

Murphy, Roland. "A Consideration of the Classification 'Wisdom Psalms.'" VTS, IX (1962), 112-140.

Osten-Sacken, P. von der. *Die Apokalyptik in ihrem Verhaltnis zu Prophetie und Weisheit.* Theologische Existenz Heute, 157. Munich, 1969.

Perdue, Leo G. *Wisdom and Cult.* SBL Dissertation Series, 30. Missoula, 1977.

Talmon, S. "Wisdom in the Book of Esther." *VT,* XIII (1963), 419-455.

AUTHOR INDEX

BIBLICAL INDEX